PEARLS GOES HOLLYWOOD

Other *Pearls Before Swine* Collections

Floundering Fathers
I Scream, You Scream, We All Scream Because Puns Suck
Stephan's Web
I'm Only in This for Me
King of the Comics
Breaking Stephan
Rat's Wars
Unsportsmanlike Conduct
Because Sometimes You Just Gotta Draw a Cover with Your Left Hand
Larry in Wonderland
When Pigs Fly
50,000,000 Pearls Fans Can't Be Wrong
The Saturday Evening Pearls
Macho Macho Animals
The Sopratos
Da Brudderhood of Zeeba Zeeba Eata
The Ratvolution Will Not Be Televised
Nighthogs
This Little Piggy Stayed Home
BLTs Taste So Darn Good

Treasuries

Pearls Takes a Wrong Turn
Pearls Hogs the Road
Pearls Gets Sacrificed
Pearls Falls Fast
Pearls Freaks the #%# Out*
Pearls Blows Up
Pearls Sells Out
The Crass Menagerie
Lions and Tigers and Crocs, Oh My!
Sgt. Piggy's Lonely Hearts Club Comic

Gift Books

Friends Should Know When They're Not Wanted
Da Crockydile Book o' Frendsheep

Kids' Books

Suit Your Selfie
When Crocs Fly
Skip School, Fly to Space
The Croc Ate My Homework
Beginning Pearls

PEARLS GOES HOLLYWOOD

STEPHAN PASTIS

A *Pearls Before Swine* Treasury

Andrews McMeel
PUBLISHING®

Pearls Before Swine is distributed internationally by Andrews McMeel Syndication.

Pearls Goes Hollywood copyright © 2020 by Stephan Pastis. All rights reserved. Printed in China. No part of this book may be used or reproduced in any manner whatsoever without written permission except in the case of reprints in the context of reviews.

Andrews McMeel Publishing
a division of Andrews McMeel Universal
1130 Walnut Street, Kansas City, Missouri 64106

www.andrewsmcmeel.com

20 21 22 23 24 SDB 10 9 8 7 6 5 4 3 2 1

ISBN: 978-1-5248-5561-1

Library of Congress Control Number: 2019943829

Pearls Before Swine can be viewed on the internet at www.pearlscomic.com.

These strips appeared in newspapers from March 12, 2017, to September 30, 2018.

Editor: Lucas Wetzel

Creative Directors: Julie Phillips and Tim Lynch

Photographer: Kenny Johnson

Cover, Inside Cover Art: Donna Oatney

Title Design: Holly Swayne

Text Design: Spencer Williams

Production Manager: Chuck Harper

Production Editor: Amy Strassner

Makeup and Wardrobe Stylist: Ashley Maurin Rodden

Assistant: Max Wagner

Dedication

To Tom McCarthy

Introduction

Two movie moguls.

Both sitting on the roof-deck of a hip hotel in West Hollywood, California.

One was actor/writer/director Tom McCarthy. Cowriter of the Pixar classic *Up*. Writer and director of *The Station Agent*, *The Visitor*, *Win Win*, *The Cobbler*, and most recently, *Spotlight*, which had won the Academy Award for Best Picture, and for which he had won the Oscar for Best Original Screenplay. And that's to say nothing of the 40 or so TV shows and movies he's acted in.

The other mogul was me.

Who in seventh grade filmed his cousins wrestling in his uncle's backyard, and in fifth grade received his elementary school's prize for "Best Posture."

I was on that roof-deck in West Hollywood because Tom had read my middle-grade book, *Timmy Failure: Mistakes Were Made*, and was considering turning it into a screenplay. And maybe one day a movie.

Until I threw a Stephan-sized wrench into everything.

"I want to write it with you," I said from my cushy deck chair, wearing sunglasses to befit my mogul status.

He stared at me for what he'd probably say was about two seconds. I believe it was closer to 10 minutes. The truth may lie somewhere in between.

"Have you ever written a movie before?" he asked.

Good question, I thought. Then answered no.

"So what do you know about writing movies?" he asked.

"Nothing," I said, wishing he'd stop asking relevant questions.

"But I read some of those books," I explained. "You know, those screenwriting books everyone reads. I can't remember the titles."

That answer so impressed him that he said nothing.

Instead, he just looked at his phone. And appeared to read a text.

I think it was from his manager.

"I'm downstairs," his manager no doubt texted him. "Ready to come up and throw the turd off the roof. We'll blame the wind."

Because in Hollywood they can make you disappear just like that.

No matter how many times you've won Best Posture.

And because in Hollywood, the writer of the original book is rarely involved in the movie. For a number of good reasons.

First, he's probably never written a film. (Check.)

Second, he might be too precious about his book. (Check.)

Third, he's an obnoxious turd. (That's just specific to me. But yes. Double check.)

So I waited for the McCarthy goons to run up to the roof-deck and throw me off. Only they didn't.

Instead, he politely said goodbye, and I walked up the street to eat pancakes by myself at IHOP.

Because eating pancakes alone is the best thing to do when you've just blown everything.

And I called my wife, Staci.

"Well, at least he didn't throw you off the roof," she said, with an indifference bordering on disappointment.

"Yeah," I answered. "But he's probably not gonna work on the movie now."

"Nothing you can do," she said. "Hey, are you gonna take Julia to school tomorrow?"

"Yeah," I said.

So I took off my sunglasses and flew home.

And back to my normal life I went. My status as movie mogul short-lived.

And weeks passed. And then months.

Months of taking my kids to school. And months of eating pancakes.

And then one day I got a call. From Tom McCarthy.

"I took a stab at writing the opening 30 pages of the film," he said. "Do you want to try writing a scene?"

"Yes," I said. "Most definitely. Wait, really?"

"Yeah," he answered, probably regretting it.

I had about a thousand questions I wanted to ask. About the film. About his writing the film. About the structure of the screenplay.

But I wasn't going to risk blowing it a second time. And I was tired of eating pancakes.

So I read what he'd written so far and reread those screenplay books and got started.

And I guess what I wrote was okay. Because after I emailed it to him, he asked me to write more.

And so began a two-year journey with Tom McCarthy.

Talking to each other almost every day. Sometimes multiple times a day. On the phone. In New York. Outlining. Writing. Rewriting. And rewriting.

A film education that I probably should have paid for. But for which I was being paid. All taught by an experienced writer and director who showed patience with me long after he should have just pushed me off that roof.

And when we were done, Disney agreed to make it into a film.

A film directed by Tom.

Who invited me to the set, where for five months in Canada and Oregon, I got to work with him and his crew, of whom I asked about a million questions and never once got pushed off a roof.

(Though I did once fall asleep on the set, my snoring ruining an otherwise good take.)

. . . .

I keep a framed photo in the room where I draw.

It's of me and Tom on the Hawthorne Bridge in Portland. It was the second to last day of the production and we had shut down the bridge one night for a shot in the film.

I keep it on my wall because I think it's about the proudest I've ever been.

Mr. Best Picture and Best Posture.

Two movie moguls.

Now friends.

Stephan Pastis
March 2020

"Love me for who I am." Perfect opening for this new treasury.
Keep that in mind when I say all the stupid stuff I'm about to say.

My new book editor, Lucas Wetzel, says that the comment below the last strip is a bad way to open a new treasury. But he's new. So to heck with Lucas Wetzel.

This "Rat Is President" storyline dates back to the last treasury. So let me fill you in: Rat is president.

I have trouble drawing shoes, so I hide them under pants. That was not possible in the second panel. Feel free to draw in better ones.

I posted this strip on both Facebook and Instagram.

13

This is all true. Bill Amend made fun of *Pearls*, so I got my hands on his original art and changed all the dialogue. I will say for the record that he does not play *World of Warcraft* 18 hours a day. He plays more. Take that, you lazy little weasel.

HEY, PIG, MY FRIEND ARTIE IS COMING TO JOIN US, BUT HE'S A LITTLE SENSITIVE RIGHT NOW BECAUSE HE JUST BLEW THE LAST SHOT OF HIS BASKETBALL GAME.

OKAY. I WON'T BRING IT UP.

HI, GUYS, WHAT ARE YOU EATING?

ARTICHOKES.

ARRRRRRGGGH!!!

SOME GUYS JUST DON'T LIKE VEGETABLES.

HEY, LISTEN TO THAT, PIG...IT SOUNDS LIKE THE ICE CREAM TRUCK.

THE ICE CREAM TRUCK! THE ICE CREAM TRUCK!

HEY, KIDS, IT'S BEER!

MORE REFRESHING THAN ICE CREAM!

THAT'S WRONG ON SO MANY LEVELS.

BEER-SICLES! BEER-SICLES!

Surely this exists. Though perhaps not marketed directly to children.

RAT THE PRESIDENT

I'VE DECIDED I'M GONNA START RUNNING THIS COUNTRY LIKE A SHERIFF IN THE OLD WEST...WITH FRONTIER JUSTICE AND HANGIN'S.

IS THAT THING REAL?

NO. IT'S JUST A PROP.

FAKE NOOSE! SAD!

I BURIED HIM ON BOOT HILL.

Fun Fact: I've been to the real Boothill in Tombstone, Arizona. (Note: There will be more "Fun Facts" like this throughout the treasury. As you'll see, they're almost never fun. But you've already bought the book.)

Rat has appeared in an actual *B.C.* comic strip, the original of which the current creators were kind enough to send me. (Though they spelled my name "Stephen" instead of "Stephan.") That's okay, I'm grateful to Masin and Mik all the same.

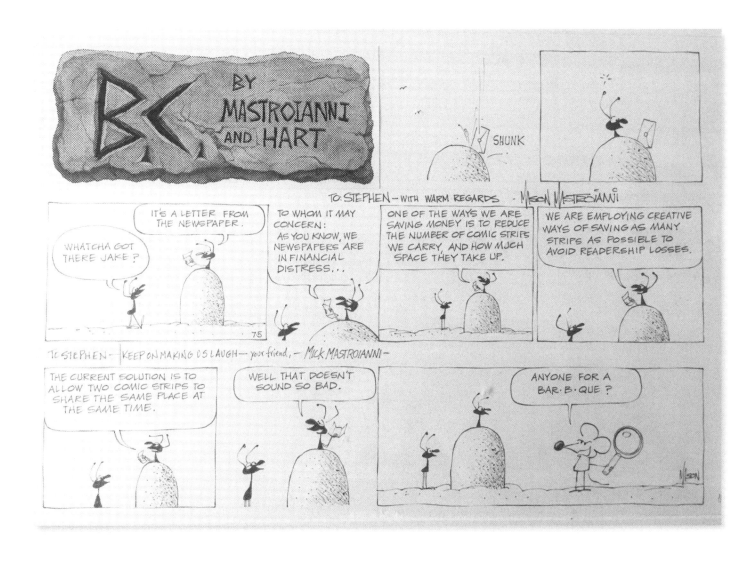

I thought this was pretty clever. And yes, I just complimented myself. Because a compliment is a compliment.

17

IT'S NOT FAIR THAT WE ALWAYS HAVE DEATH HANGING OVER US.

IT'S THIS GREAT RANDOM UNKNOWN. AND IT'S NOT RIGHT. I WANT TO KNOW HOW I DIE. WHEN I DIE.

I DON'T THINK THAT'S POSSIBLE.

WELL, IT IS NOW. BECAUSE I'VE INVENTED THE B.M.I.

B.M.I.?

BALLOON MORTALITY INDICATOR. YOU BLINDFOLD YOURSELF AND THROW A DART AGAINST THAT FENCE. THE BALLOON YOU HIT INDICATES YOUR FATE.

FLU 2061

HEART ATTACK 2021

HIT BY TRAIN 2040

DROWNED AT SEA 2057

TRAMPLED BY BULLS 2035

CAN I TRY?

SURE.

WOOOSH

HEY, GUYS, WHAT ARE YOU—OHHHH GOD

FLU 2061

HIT BY TRAIN 2040

DROWNED AT SEA 2057

TR B TRA 20

WELL, WE KNOW HOW GOAT DIES.

YOU'RE RIGHT. HOW EERIE.

OHH..

I don't have an exact count on the total number of characters that have died in *Pearls*, but I'm pretty sure it's higher than that of *Peanuts*.

18

Sometimes I record Warriors games to watch later. Then my idiot best friend will text me during the game and say, "Whoa. The Warriors are really blowing it, aren't they?" I think the lesson here is to never have friends.

You read it the sad way, didn't you?

Okay, how is the rest of the horse's big body fitting under that blanket? I guess he really is sick. Or someone doesn't know how to draw. I'll blame the horse.

Answer No. 11: If you look at the blue sleeve on the right, you'll see I signed the strip.
I don't sign my strips. (Mostly because I want to be able to deny drawing them later.)

Louis really did tell me that one. So if you didn't like it, blame him.

My daughter played doubles tennis with a girl named Grace. Thus, the inspiration for this one.

This really is a problem. So truly, if you can, pay for a newspaper, online or print. Because without them, we are all screwed.

I read from my e-reader when I'm lying in bed at night. But when I get sleepy, I sometimes lose my grip and drop it on my face. Occasionally, it leaves a mark, and when people ask me what happened, I have to say, "I hurt myself reading."

Maybe we should have a strict rule that we only eat animals who would eat us, like lions, tigers, crocodiles, and pigs. And yes, I know pigs don't eat humans, but I really like bacon, so I'm including them.

24

Not many people know this, but playing the game Operation is the only training doctors get in medical school.

Joke explanation: Communists from the former Soviet Union were often called "Reds." And the fellow you see in the second panel is a communist from the Soviet Union. Thus, he is waving a Red flag. And if it were still 1975, you'd find this joke hilarious.

I'm with Rat here. It's very depressing to think that the world will one day go on without me. I'm hoping to be immortal and avoid that.

E.T. A movie from the 1980s. A time when the Soviet Union was still in existence. I'm starting to think all of my references are to really old things from 30 years ago.

Okay, fine, *The Godfather Part II* was from 1974, but the first Lord of the Rings film was from 2001. So I am now hip and current.

Since these answers are no longer on Facebook, I will give you the 23 teams here: 1) Giants; 2) Browns; 3) Bills; 4) Chargers (Charge her); 5) Chiefs; 6) Rams; 7) Eagles; 8) Titans; 9) Cardinals; 10) Saints; 11) Bears; 12) Steelers (Steal her); 13) Raiders (Raid her); 14) Vikings; 15) Packers (Pack her); 16) Lions (Lyin'); 17) Jets; 18) Dolphins; 19) Redskins; 20) Broncos; 21) Jaguars; 22) Falcons; 23) Patriots. (The one that most people seemed to miss was the Lions.)

Fun Fact: I go to the gym twice a week. I lift weights for 30 minutes and run for 30 minutes. That makes me the only cartoonist in the world who exercises.

I am now told by my editor, Lucas Wetzel, that there are other cartoonists who exercise. That's too bad, because I like to think of myself as extraordinary.

For some odd reason, I somehow forgot to add the dot shading to this strip (like the kind you see on the next strip on the countertop and the seats). I don't think I've ever done that before. I note, however, that the date of the strip is April 20, a date when marijuana is celebrated. So I'm gonna say I was high.

Eating cheese puffs is a great thing to do when you're high. That, and forgetting to add dot shading to your strip.

[Note from Stephan's editor, Lucas Wetzel, in regard to the last two comments: Though it may be legal in some states, Andrews McMeel Publishing does not endorse the use of marijuana. Booze, however, is fine. We drink lots of booze.]

4/23

That last guy has serious problems. With any luck, his orb will plunge off a cliff.

Always read the fine print.

I spent a night in Mobile, Alabama, recently. I drank beer and went to bed.

It's commentary like this that makes me think I should write travel guides.

We used to have a hamster. But one day, he got out of his cage and disappeared. I like to think he's living in a condo in Miami.

I recently put this "No Soliciting" sign on my front door to keep telemarketers and others from bothering me. But the little "thank you" at the bottom really bugs me. What am I thanking them for? Trying to bother me and failing? I wanted one that just ended with, "You scum-sucking toads." But apparently, they don't make it.

I'm rather amazed I got away with Goat's line in the second to last panel, given that it so clearly telegraphs the word "sh*t." That would not have been okay when the strip started in newspapers back in 2002. Clearly, there is a bit more leeway now.

So remember, kids, violence *is* the answer.

[Note from the legal department of Andrews McMeel Publishing in regard to the last comment: Violence is never the answer. Though booze sometimes is. We drink lots and lots of booze.]

HEY, RAT, HOW COME YOU'RE NOT HERE?

STUCK IN TRAFFIC...EITHER THERE'S A WRECK JUST AHEAD, OR THERE ARE JUST TOO MANY PEOPLE DRIVING RIGHT NOW, IN WHICH CASE IT COULD BE LIKE THIS THE WHOLE WAY.

WAIT...WAIT...IT'S A BIG WRECK!! YESSSS!!

SOMEWHERE WE LOST OUR HUMANITY.

I don't know about you, but this really is a feeling I get, because it means the traffic will most likely clear up just beyond the accident. And in the event you don't share that feeling and I'm just a sociopath, please forget I said anything.

WHEN YOU PAY AT A GROCERY STORE, IS IT YOUR RESPONSIBILITY TO PUT THE DIVIDER IN FRONT OF YOUR FOOD OR BEHIND IT?

BEHIND.

IN FRONT.

CRACK

I LIKE TO THINK I'M CREATING A BETTER WORLD.

I always feel profound guilt when I haven't put down a divider and the person behind me has to put it down to separate their groceries from mine. So now I solve that by putting the little chain across the checkout line that says, "This register closed."

WHO'S THAT WOMAN, GOAT?

SHE'S THE SUPER OF MY BUILDING. SHE'S POSING FOR A PHOTO SHOOT TO BE USED IN OUR BUILDING BROCHURE.

SO SHE'S A MODEL?

YEAH. AND I'M ACTUALLY DATING HER.

WHO'S GOAT DATING?

A SUPER MODEL.

STUPID STEPHAN PUN?

HOW ELSE COULD GOAT DATE A SUPERMODEL?

I CAN HEAR YOU, YOU KNOW.

WHAT ARE YOU DOING, RAT?

I'M HEALING AMERICA BY PUTTING THESE TWO PEOPLE IN A BOX TOGETHER.

BOX O' RECONCILIATION

JOE IS A FOX NEWS-WATCHING, CRACKER BARREL-EATING CONSERVATIVE.

BOX RECONC

DAVID IS A NEW YORK TIMES-READING, WHOLE FOODS-SHOPPING LIBERAL.

RECONCILIATION

BY PUTTING THEM TOGETHER, I'M FORCING EACH OF THEM TO SEE THAT THE OTHER IS A HUMAN BEING, AND NOT SOME MONSTER.

DO YOU THINK IT'LL WORK?

I DO. BECAUSE BEING TOGETHER WILL FORCE THEM TO HAVE A FRANK EXCHANGE OF—

5/7

BOX O' RECONCILIATION

HAND GRENADES.

COMMIE.

FASCIST.

HEY! NO KILLING IN THE BOX O' RECONCILIATION.

Rat's line in the last panel, "No killing in the Box O' Reconciliation," is a play on the famous line from the movie *Dr. Strangelove*, "You can't fight in here. This is the War Room."

I was recently told by someone that my jeans are too saggy, so I bought tighter ones. But I have very skinny legs and it looks weird. So now I no longer leave home.

I can guarantee you that at some future book signing, a disgruntled parent will come up to me and say, "Thanks to you, my kid now knows the term 'G-spot.'" I never know what to say to them, other than, "You're very welcome."

WHAT ARE YOU DOING, PIG?

TRYING TO RECORD SOMETHING ON THIS MICROPHONE, BUT I HAVE TO AVOID ALL WORDS THAT START WITH 'P' BECAUSE THEY CAUSE A POPPING SOUND.

THAT'S WHY YOU PUT ON THIS LITTLE POP FILTER. IT PREVENTS THAT.

SO YOU'RE SAYING THAT NOW I CAN TRY SAYING 'P'?

ALL I AM SAYING IS GIVE P's A CHANCE.

EVEN I HATE YOU NOW.

WHY DO CREATIVE PEOPLE CREATE?

I THINK THEY NEED THE ATTENTION THAT COMES FROM AN AUDIENCE TO FILL A LONG-STANDING NEED FOR ACCEPTANCE AND ADMIRATION.

HOLD ME.

SO THEY'RE LIKE STRIPPERS, BUT MORE PATHETIC.

FINE, I'LL TAKE MY TOP OFF.

All that working out is really paying off.

Dear Pig,
Hope you have a wonderful day! You're handsome! You're smart! And all the women love you!

WELL, THAT SURE IS A NICE LETTER TO GET. WHO SENT IT?

ME.

I FIGURE IT STILL COUNTS.

It appears that some lazy cartoonist just drew that envelope once and then cut-and-pasted it three times. I will try to find out who's responsible and get back to you.

38

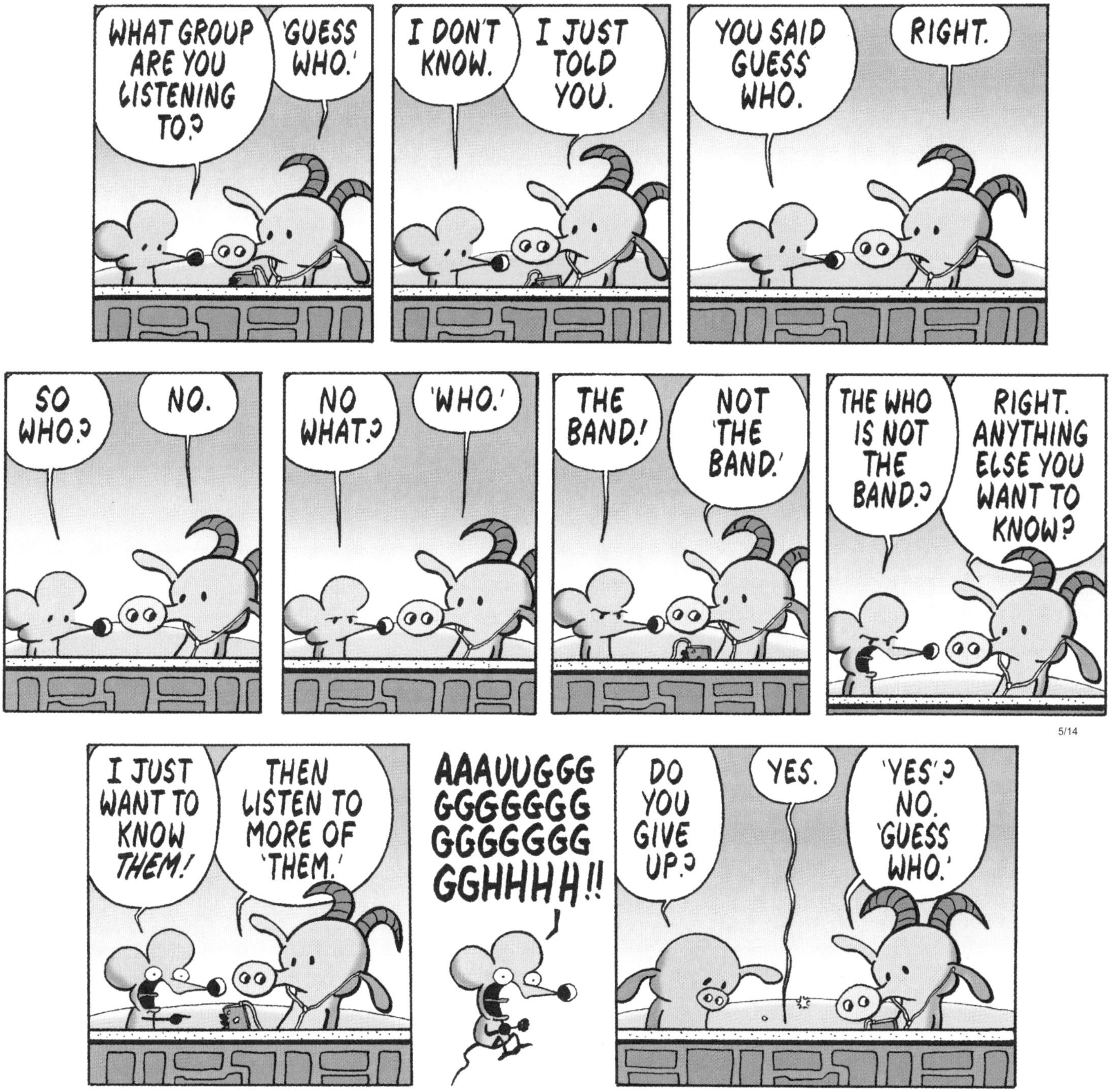
WHAT GROUP ARE YOU LISTENING TO?
'GUESS WHO.'
I DON'T KNOW.
I JUST TOLD YOU.
YOU SAID GUESS WHO.
RIGHT.
SO WHO?
NO.
NO WHAT?
'WHO.'
THE BAND!
NOT 'THE BAND.'
THE WHO IS NOT THE BAND?
RIGHT. ANYTHING ELSE YOU WANT TO KNOW?
I JUST WANT TO KNOW *THEM!*
THEN LISTEN TO MORE OF 'THEM.'
AAAUUGGG GGGGGGG GGGGGGG GGHHHH!!
DO YOU GIVE UP?
YES.
'YES'? NO. 'GUESS WHO.'

5/14

WHAT DID YOU GET YOUR MOM FOR MOTHER'S DAY?

NOTHING. I DON'T CELEBRATE CONVENTIONAL 'HALLMARK' HOLIDAYS. INSTEAD, I MARK MY OWN MEANINGFUL DAYS ON THE CALENDAR.

LIKE WHAT?

LIKE TODAY— MAY 15. 'GET AS DRUNK AS YOU CAN' DAY.

I'LL STICK TO TEA.

PLEASE. RESPECT MY CULTURAL TRADITIONS.

IN AN EFFORT TO MINIMIZE THE IMPACT OF ALL THE IDIOTS IN THE WORLD, I DECLARE TODAY, MAY 16, 'TRY NOT TO BE AS STUPID AS YOU NORMALLY ARE' DAY.

I DON'T LIKE TO THINK OF ANYONE AS IDIOTS, BECAUSE I THINK EVERY SINGLE HUMAN ON EARTH HAS VALUE AND SOMETHING TO CONTRIBUTE.

I SEE YOU'RE NOT OBSERVING THE HOLIDAY.

This holiday should happen more than once a year.

PIG, IF WE'RE GONNA STAY TOGETHER, YOU'RE GONNA HAVE TO CHANGE.

THAT'S THE LAST STRAW.

FINE. WE'RE BREAKING UP.

JUST BECAUSE YOU TOOK THE LAST STRAW IN THE DISPENSER?

NEVER MIND.

YOU'RE VERY FICKLE. NOW I WANT TO BREAK UP.

That's supposed to be a straw dispenser, but now I'm thinking it looks more like a napkin dispenser. Perhaps I should avoid all jokes about dispensers.

I GOT A JOB AT A 'NOT FOR PROFIT' CAFE.

WELL, GOOD FOR YOU. WHAT CHARITY DO THEY DONATE THEIR REVENUES TO?

NONE. THEY JUST DON'T MAKE A PROFIT.

RIGHT.

AND IF THEY DID, THEY SURE WOULDN'T GIVE IT TO A DUMB CHARITY.

THE PAPER SAYS THERE ARE A LOT OF RELIGIOUS SECTS IN OUR CITY WHO SHOULD REALLY HAVE ROUND-THE-CLOCK SECURITY PROTECTION.

DO THEY?

NO. VERY FEW OF THEM CAN AFFORD IT.

WOW. WE HAVE A LOT OF UNPROTECTED SECTS.

STOP!

IT'S A HUGE RISK.

WOULD IT BE BETTER TO HAVE NO SECTS AT ALL?

I really liked this joke. Good thing I didn't have to ruin it by drawing a dispenser.

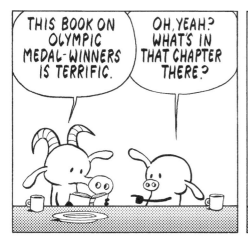

THIS BOOK ON OLYMPIC MEDAL-WINNERS IS TERRIFIC.

OH, YEAH? WHAT'S IN THAT CHAPTER THERE?

MARK SPITZ.

ON WHAT?

NOTHING.

DOES THAT REALLY DESERVE A MEDAL?

Fun Fact: When I was a kid, I snuck into some equestrian event in the 1984 Summer Olympics in Los Angeles. I didn't have the money for a ticket and just wanted to be able to say I went to the Olympics. Security was a bit more lax in those days.

This really is a creepy thought.

42

This strip and the next one were both references to Barnum & Bailey announcing that they were shutting down their circus.

I cannot resist Fritos. If you put a bag of them in front of me, I will only stop eating if someone literally grabs the bag and hides it from me. That someone is usually my wife. And even then, I'll go searching for it.

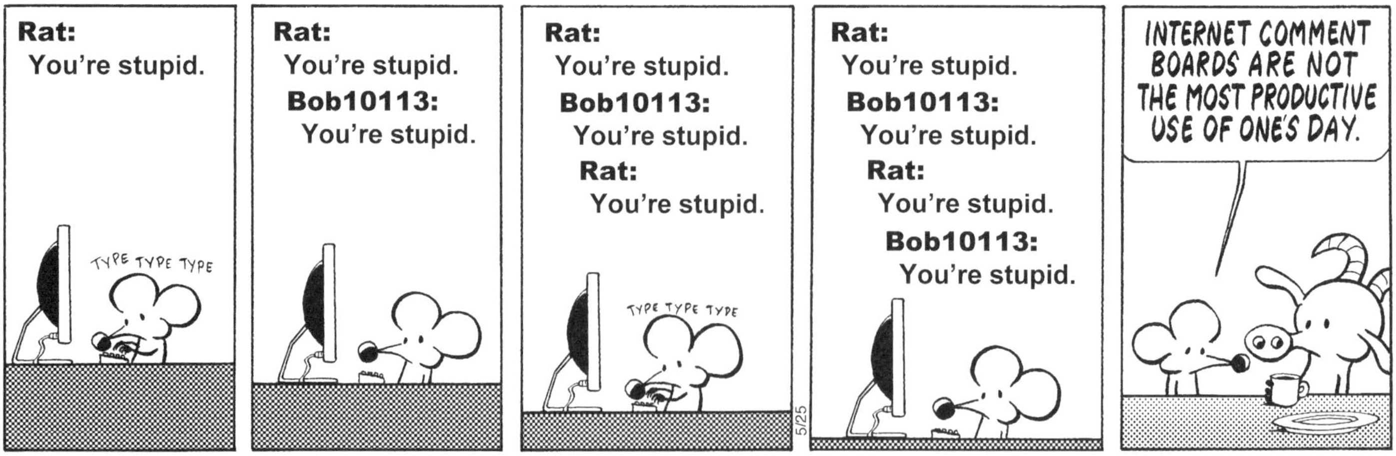
Rat:
You're stupid.
TYPE TYPE TYPE
Rat:
You're stupid.
Bob10113:
You're stupid.
Rat:
You're stupid.
Bob10113:
You're stupid.
Rat:
You're stupid.
TYPE TYPE TYPE
5/25
Rat:
You're stupid.
Bob10113:
You're stupid.
Rat:
You're stupid.
Bob10113:
You're stupid.
INTERNET COMMENT BOARDS ARE NOT THE MOST PRODUCTIVE USE OF ONE'S DAY.

I have no trouble ignoring any and all comments written about my strip on the internet. For me, they are the opposite of Fritos.

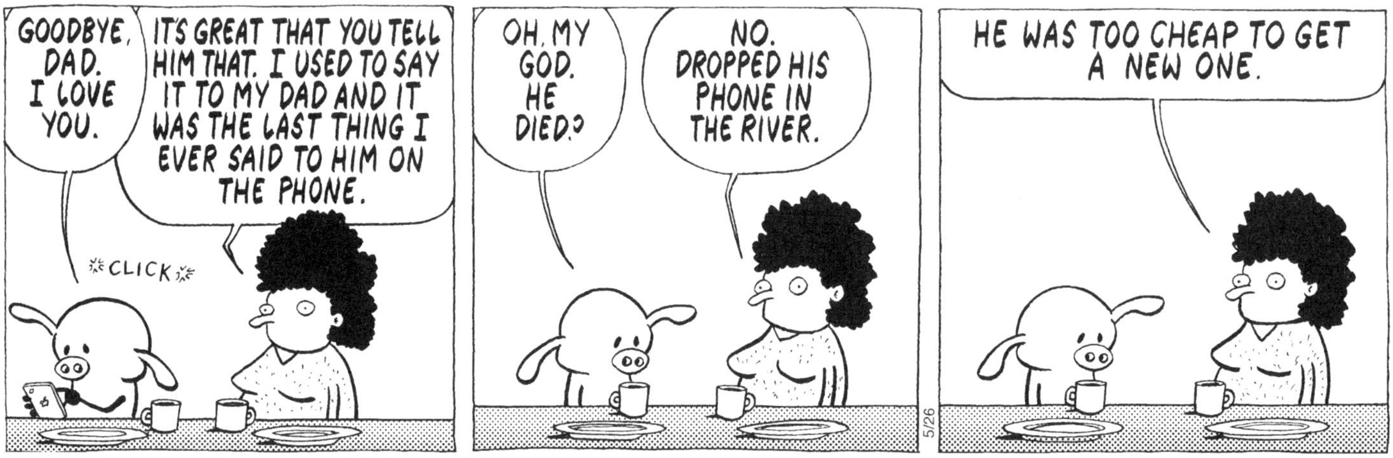
GOODBYE, DAD. I LOVE YOU.
IT'S GREAT THAT YOU TELL HIM THAT. I USED TO SAY IT TO MY DAD AND IT WAS THE LAST THING I EVER SAID TO HIM ON THE PHONE.
CLICK
OH, MY GOD. HE DIED?
NO. DROPPED HIS PHONE IN THE RIVER.
5/26
HE WAS TOO CHEAP TO GET A NEW ONE.

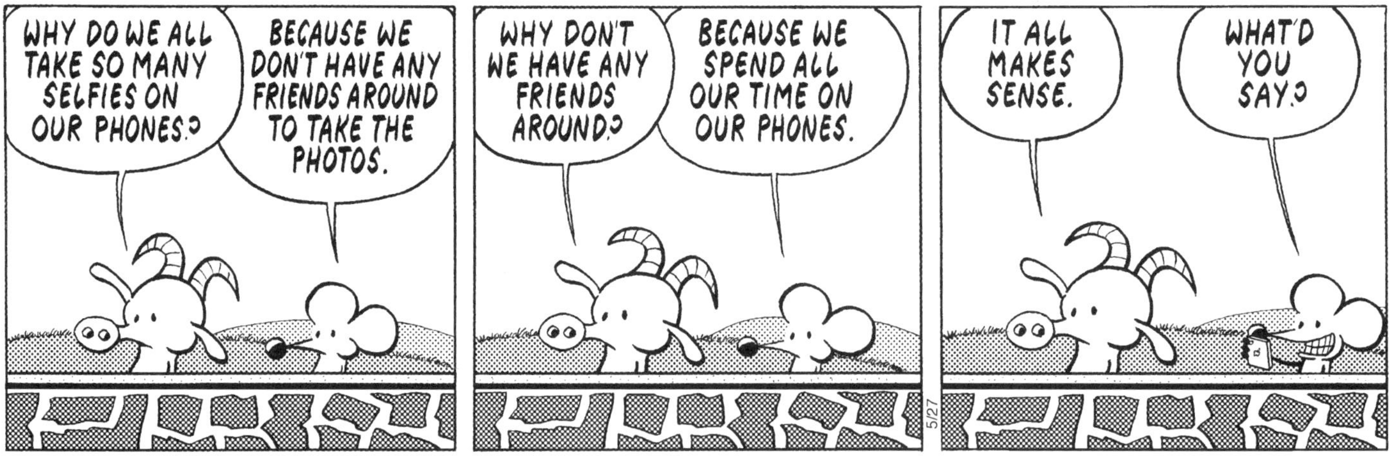
WHY DO WE ALL TAKE SO MANY SELFIES ON OUR PHONES?
BECAUSE WE DON'T HAVE ANY FRIENDS AROUND TO TAKE THE PHOTOS.
WHY DON'T WE HAVE ANY FRIENDS AROUND?
BECAUSE WE SPEND ALL OUR TIME ON OUR PHONES.
5/27
IT ALL MAKES SENSE.
WHAT'D YOU SAY?

This doesn't apply to me. I had no friends even *before* smartphones.

If that painting of the horse is the best that guy can do, he should stop painting and watch cat videos.

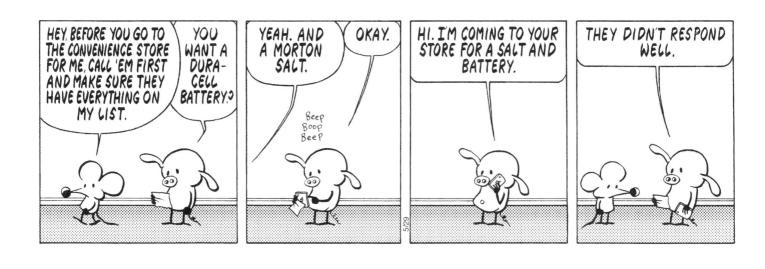

It's hard not to watch your total number of followers. I check it way too many times a day.

Draw Pig. Add hair. Add necklace. Boom. You have Pigita.

Repressed Childhood Memory That Just Came to My Head That I Haven't Thought About in 40 Years: When I was a little kid and I was home for the summer, I used to lie in the entryway just below the mail slot by the front door. The mailman would put the mail in the slot, and it would all fall on my head. For reasons I can't explain, I enjoyed that.

I can't believe I'm about to admit this, but here goes. I was on a date in college. After, I went to the girl's house. Her parents weren't home. I had to go to the bathroom, and I used her parents' bathroom. I clogged the toilet. The dirty water overflowed and filled the bathroom. With little choice, I grabbed her parents' monogrammed towels and used them to clean it up. Everything smelled. Trapped and humiliated, I made up an excuse for why I had to leave and fled the house, never to see the girl again. (And you thought the mail slot thing was bad.)

Leave it to me to run a Christmas joke in early June.

WHERE WERE YOU TODAY? — READING THIS BOOK BY A DOCTOR WHO KEPT TRYING UNSUCCESSFULLY TO EUTHANIZE A HORSE.

I COULDN'T PUT IT DOWN.

THAT WAS THE BOOK TITLE, WASN'T IT? — YEAH. SOMEONE REIN ME IN.

YOU JUST REACHED FOR THOSE CHIPS WITH YOUR HAND WHEN YOU COULD HAVE VERY EASILY USED THOSE TONGS. — I DIDN'T SEE YOU THERE.

SO? — SO LOOK AT THE DEFINITION OF TONGS...

tongs *noun*

the things you use only when others are looking

HOW COMFORTING. — REMEMBER— 'IF NO ONE'S THERE, TOUCHING'S FAIR.'

Oh, man. Another admission. I rarely use the tongs. I'm the guy who just reaches in figuring I can grab the cheese cube without touching any of the others, but of course I do. I'm sorry. Never follow me in a buffet line. And never let me use your parents' bathroom.

WHAT ARE YOU DOING, DAD? — Playing lottery. Larry teeket got all six numbers dis time.

DAD, THE ODDS OF YOU WINNING THAT ARE ABOUT ONE IN FOURTEEN MILLION. THAT MEANS YOU'D HAVE TO BUY 1,000 TICKETS A DAY FOR THE NEXT 40 YEARS TO HAVE AN EVEN CHANCE. DO YOU UNDERSTAND WHAT THAT MEANS? — Yeah. It mean Larry stoopid.

WELL, IT DOESN'T MAKE YOU STUPID. IT JUST MEANS— — Larry got go store. Buy 999 more teekets.

NO. — Hey, woomun, household budget gonna change.

One time in Sea Ranch, California, I walked into the grocery store and bought one of those scratch-off lottery tickets and won 10 dollars. Thinking it was my lucky grocery store, I have since gone there at least 50 more times to buy lottery tickets. I have lost every single time.

My wife, Staci, does not like us to use the heater. She is very cheap. I can say that because I'm pretty sure she doesn't read these commentaries.

If in fact Staci *does* read these commentaries, let me say here that she is thrifty, not cheap, and that I love her very much.

6/11

When I was a little kid, I vacationed in Hawaii with my best friend Emilio. When his mother was gone, we threw slices of bologna off our 32nd-floor balcony. It was a bit of a science experiment. Turns out gravity causes bologna to fall.

If you caught that error in the first panel on your own, you really should be an editor. Almost everyone misses it.

For those of you who are under 30, Rat is dressed up as Carnac the Magnificent in that last panel. It's a character that used to be played by *Tonight Show* host Johnny Carson.

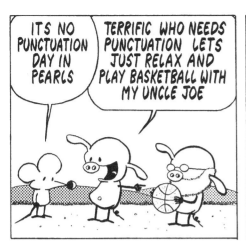

Apparently, Rat is armed at all times. Not quite sure where he keeps the gun.

Sadly, the manufacturers of Maker's Mark bourbon did not send me any free samples for this exquisite product placement.

53

I got the words "erectile" and "orgasm" into the same panel in a Sunday comic strip.
That's some groundbreaking shit.

54

Regarding the comment below the last strip: That is the first time I have ever sworn in one of these books. Because I am not done being groundbreaking.

Maybe I should admit here that it took me 45 minutes to draw that dartboard and it still looks terrible. Mental note: Do not write jokes about dartboards.

THE CHURCH IS THINKING ABOUT CANONIZING THIS OLD WOMAN WHO HELPED THE POOR.

HOW SAD.

WHY IS THAT SAD?

THEY'RE SHOOTING HER OUT OF A CANNON.

LET'S START OVER.

SO MUCH FOR BEING KIND.

6/22

I THINK THE WAR ON DRUGS FAILED BECAUSE OF THE WHOLE 'JUST SAY NO' CAMPAIGN.

BECAUSE IT WAS TOO SIMPLISTIC?

BECAUSE ALL THE DRUG DEALERS HAD TO DO WAS FRAME THE QUESTION RIGHT....HERE, WATCH.... HEY YOU, DO YOU NOT WANT ANY DRUGS?

NO.

HA! THAT'S A YES! AND NOW YOU'RE HOOKED ON DRUGS!

I SHOULD REALLY BE DRUG CZAR.

NO.

6/23

The "Just Say No" campaign was spearheaded by President Ronald Reagan's wife, Nancy. Reagan was a big fan of Charles Schulz's comic strip *Peanuts*. None of that has anything to do with anything, but sometimes I run out of things to say.

HI, PROFESSOR PETE...ARE YOU STILL TEACHING TYPING AT THE HIGH SCHOOL?

NO. GOT BURNED OUT. SO I THOUGHT I'D TAKE A BREAK AND TRY TO WRITE THE NEXT GREAT AMERICAN NOVEL.

CAN I SEE WHAT YOU HAVE SO FAR?

The quick brown fox jumps over the lazy dog.

THAT'S WHERE I GOT STUCK.

6/24

The sentence in the third panel is something they used to make people type in typing classes because it involves every single letter of the alphabet.

I used to go on the Wikipedia page of another syndicated cartoonist and change his bio to cite me as the biggest cartooning influence of his life.

HEY, STEPH, WHAT DO YOU THINK IS THE KEY TO WRITING A GOOD JOKE?

I THINK IT'S ALL IN HOW YOU FRAME IT.

NOPE. STILL STUPID.

The frame in the third panel was drawn by my daughter, Julia, marking the first time she has ever drawn something in my strip. If you look really closely, you can find her name in the frame.

Dear Pope, I would like to be named a saint.

You may ask why I should be considered for this high honor. And I'll tell you.

Because as a saint, I think I'd be less likely to punch idiots.

OH, GOOD.

'UNLESS YOU THINK THERE IS ROOM FOR A PUNCHING SAINT.'

I recently went to the Vatican but was not personally greeted by the pope. You'd think with my stature, he'd hang out with me, maybe even get a beer. But no. He made no effort.

WHERE'S RAT TODAY?

PUTTING DOWN HIS HORSE.

OH, MY GOD, NO! WHY?

YOU'RE FAT, YOU'RE DUMB, AND YOU'RE LAZY.

I THINK HE JUST LIKES PUTTING HIM DOWN.

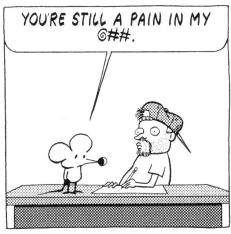

Oh, man, I miss Borders. It was a great big bookstore that had a café and also sold music.

I have dictated text messages to my wife, Staci, and not bothered to look at them before clicking send. In trying to tell her I was coming home very soon, I've said stuff like, "Coming home no. Fat."

7/2

I recently went to Mexico City for two weeks. While there, I did an event for the State Department and got to spend an hour with the U.S. Ambassador to Mexico. Three months later, she resigned. I like to think my visit pushed her over the edge.

I will admit that from time to time I take photos of my food. But only when it's really good and only to send to my best friend Emilio because it makes him jealous and hungry.

You can't beat the double finger point. I do it sometimes after I've told a joke. Mostly because it mortifies my kids.

RAT THE PRESIDENT

YOU SHOULD BE AWARE THAT I FIRED MY LAST ADVISOR BECAUSE HE MADE A DUMB 'FAKE NOOSE' PUN.

YESSIR, I WON'T MAKE A JOKE ABOUT A NOOSE OR ANY- THING ELSE.

THAT'S THE BEST THING I'VE HEARD ALL WEEK.

SO NO NOOSE IS GOOD NOOSE?

I RAN HIM OVER WITH AIR FORCE ONE.

HEY, GOAT, I'D LIKE YOU TO MEET MY FRIEND... HE'S AN EMBEDDED REPORTER.

OH, WOW. THOSE GUYS GO TO IRAQ AND SYRIA. HARD TO FIND A PERSON WITH MORE GUTS THAN SOMEONE WHO'S EMBEDDED.

HEY. WANT TO BE INTERVIEWED?

NOT WHAT I WAS EXPECTING.

WILL ONE OF YOU GET ME MORE CHEESE PUFFS?

In 2009, I went on a USO visit to Iraq. The scariest moment was when I had to shower, because a sign warned of occasional electrocution. I took a very fast shower.

Woomun, me tink me want renew wedding vows.

REALLY, LARRY? THAT'S SO ROMANTIC. WHY?

Becuss me tink me got bad deal da first time.

Woomun tuff negoshiator.

Contrary to popular belief, I am still married and have been since 1993. Though perhaps that will end after cheap Staci reads some of these comments.

HAMMY HAMSTER SAVED UP ALL HER MONEY TO TAKE HER KIDS TO EUROPE.

WE'LL SEE ALL THE GREAT CITIES.

YAY!

WE'LL VISIT ALL THE MUSEUMS.

YAY!

WE'LL SAMPLE ALL THE CUISINE.

YAY!

BECAUSE THIS WILL BE AN ADVENTURE!

YAY!!

HAMMY'S KIDS NEVER LEFT THE HOTEL ROOM.

I'M BORED.

DOES THIS PLACE HAVE WIFI?

CAN WE EAT AT McDONALD'S?

AND THAT'S WHY HAMSTERS EAT THEIR YOUNG.

THAT SEEMS FAIR.

BUT DID THEY HAVE WIFI?!

RAT'S AT A JOB PLACEMENT AGENCY TODAY...THEY'RE TRYING TO PLACE HIM SOMEWHERE THAT'S SUITED TO HIS SKILL SET.

WHAT DID HE TELL THEM THAT WAS?

BEING HOSTILE AND RUDE AND TREATING PEOPLE HOWEVER HE WANTS, PARTICULARLY WHEN THEY'RE HELPLESS AND TRAPPED.

BUT WHAT INDUSTRY WOULD WANT THAT?

WELCOME TO OUR AIRLINE.

SO IF WE'RE OVERSOLD, CAN I PUNCH THEM IN THE FACE?

I was recently stuck on a grounded airplane for over 10 hours. It was the worst airline experience of my life. You can read about it on my blog at: https://stephanpastis.wordpress.com.

RAT THE AIRLINE GATE AGENT

HI, FOLKS, WE'RE GONNA START THE BOARDING PROCESS WITH FIRST CLASS. WELCOME ABOARD!

NEXT WILL BE OUR GOLD PREMIERE MEMBERS AND BUSINESS PLATINUM SELECT. WELCOME ABOARD!

OKAY, NOW THE REST OF YOU SCUM.

TECHNICALLY, THEY'RE STILL PEOPLE.

MOOOOO, CATTLE, MOOOOOO.

I don't know what magical thing you have to do to be included in one of these groups, but for whatever reason, I am almost always boarding last. Thus, I get the worst seat left, between a crying baby and a fat guy.

LOOK HOW MUCH THESE GUYS LOOK LIKE EACH OTHER. IT'S UNCANNY.

I'M SORRY, PIG. DO YOU KNOW WHAT THAT WORD MEANS?

HA HA. OF COURSE.

USE IT IN A SENTENCE.

I PREFER BEER IN BOTTLES BECAUSE IT TASTES UNCANNY.

UH. NO.

YOU PREFER BEER IN CANS?

The plane I was stuck on for 10 hours just might have been an airline that rhymes with Boonited, a.k.a. "The Unfriendly Skies."

That woman has a very odd head and body shape. Like the guy who drew her can't draw. It's too bad cartooning is part of cartooning.

7/16

For future generations who will long since have forgotten what this comes from, it is the Donald Trump campaign promise: "I'm building a wall and Mexico is gonna pay for it."

That cop looks like he's a member of the Village People.

Every time I see my flight has Wi-Fi, I get very excited. And every time I realize it does absolutely nothing. Except drain your phone battery. Which I guess is something.

This is what happens to your phone when you use Wi-Fi on a plane.

I have been to Tokyo twice and actually saw this happen. I often wish I had one of those sticks.

It's hard to explain this to younger people, but when I was a kid in 1977 or so, *Happy Days* was the biggest thing in the world, and Fonzie (Henry Winkler) was the biggest star. His episodes with Pinky Tuscadero in the demolition derby were all must-watch TV.

68

WHO ARE YOU TEXTING?

MY NEW GIRL-FRIEND. SHE TOLD A JOKE AND I'M SAYING 'HA.'

'HA' ISN'T A LAUGH. IT'S A RETORT.

WHAT ABOUT 'HAHA'?

SARCASTIC LAUGH.

'HAHAHA'?

MILDLY AMUSED.

'HAHAHAHA'?

ACTUAL LAUGH.

Hahahahaha

TYPE

TYPE

TYPE

TYPE

SEND

7/23

YOU JUST SENT A TEXT WITH FIVE OR MORE HA'S.

SO?

SO NOW YOU LOOK DRUNK.

MAYBE I'LL JUST THROW MY PHONE IN A RIVER.

Excuse me. But are you *drunk*?

Is the thing about the HAHA laugh just me, or does it feel sarcastic to you, too? Like the person is not really laughing, but sort of slow-clapping you.

RAT SENT US A POSTCARD FROM HIS HAWAIIAN VACATION.

OH, MAN...I WISH I COULD HAVE GONE THERE... WHAT'S IT SAY?

ME YOU

VACATIONING FRIENDS ARE THE WORST.

I should sell this as an actual postcard that people can send when they're on vacation.

WHAT'S THE MATTER, RAT?

I DON'T FEEL LIKE TALKING ABOUT IT.

WHAT'S WITH THE PASTA?

PENNE FOR YOUR THOUGHTS.

YOU DID NOT IMPROVE HIS MOOD.

RAT THE PRESIDENT

HOW ARE WE TODAY, SIR?

SAD. THE PRESS IS STILL SAYING MEAN THINGS ABOUT ME.

WELL, THAT'S THEIR FIRST AMENDMENT PRIVILEGE. IT'S RIGHT THERE IN THE BILL OF RIGHTS.

I THOUGHT YOU'D SAY THAT. SO I HAD THE NATIONAL ARCHIVES BRING ME THE ACTUAL DOCUMENT.

AND I CROSSED THAT PART OUT.

OH, LORD.

NOW IT JUST LOOKS LIKE A BIG FOUNDING FATHER BOO-BOO.

Fun Founding Fathers Fact: I have memorized the first 20 or so lines of the song "Alexander Hamilton" (from the musical *Hamilton*). If you ever have to take a long drive with me, I will sing it so many times you will want to jump from the car.

WELL, RAT, I'M AFRAID I HAVE SOME BAD NEWS. I'VE LOOKED AT YOUR ULTRASOUND AND YOUR C.T. SCAN AND IT LOOKS LIKE YOU HAVE KIDNEY STONES.

WRONG. FAKE NEWS. YOU FAIL. SAD!

HAS THE WORLD CHANGED OR IS IT ME?

WELL, I'M OFF TO TAKE A COUPLE TESTS FOR A JOB I WANT TO GET.

HANG ON, PIG. I'D LIKE YOU TO MEET ED. WE'RE BESTIES.

BESTIES?

YEAH, I'M HIS BEST FRIEND, AND HE'S MINE. AND TOGETHER, TWO BESTS MAKE BESTIES. SO WHAT DID YOU SAY YOU'RE GOING TO DO?

TAKE A COUPLE OF... TESTIES.

OKAY, WHO STARTED THIS?

NOT ME.

I CAN'T MENTION MY TWO TESTIES?

COMIC STRIP CENSOR

I'm the first person to say "testes" on a newspaper comics page. I'd like that on my tombstone.

IF THE DECLARATION OF INDEPENDENCE WERE WRITTEN TODAY.

We hold these truths to be self-evident, that all men are created equal.

Just sayin'.

IT REALLY IS A STUPID EXPRESSION.

LIKE YOUR PUNS.

JUST SAYIN'!

"Just sayin'" is my nominee for dumbest expression ever. Also, my puns are not stupid. They're geniusosity personified.

I have a bad back that hits me once or so a year. It is crazy painful and often leaves me unable to get out of bed. This is where you play the sad little violins.

Sometimes when I'm not sure people will get the pun (in this case, "perv view"), I have a character say it in the last panel. Sort of lessens the impact of the joke, but it's better than people missing the joke entirely.

The current climate of oversensitivity is really a killer for comedy. I think we'll look back on this era and wonder how things got so nuts.

I recently spent a summer in Portland, Oregon, and drove on one of these roads. I think if a cyclist is riding in front of you, you have to stay behind him, no matter how slow he's biking. It gave me lots of material for Jef the Cyclist.

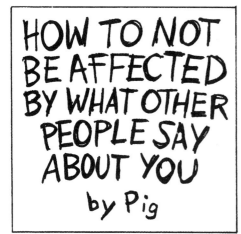

I'm so used to drawing Pig that sometimes it's hard for me to draw him badly. So I switch the pen to my left hand and grab it like you would an ice pick. That's how I drew Pig in the second panel.

74

I really should make this into a comic book.

DUDE, IT'S NOON... WHY ARE YOU STILL IN BED?

BECAUSE NOTHING THAT WILL HAPPEN TODAY WILL BE BETTER THAN THE WARMTH AND COMFORT THAT I HAVE HERE.

YOU MAY HAVE SOLVED LIFE.

This was probably the most popular strip of the year.

HEY, RAT, SAY SOMETHING RUDE TO MY ARAB PAL HERE AND SEE HOW I REACT.

HE'S FAT AND STUPID.

WHAT ARE YOU DOING?

TURNING THE OTHER SHEIKH.

MAY A CAMEL STOMP ON YOUR FAMILY JEWELS.

AH, WHAT A GLORIOUS MORNING... I'LL JUST CHECK MY TWITTER FEED AND SEE WHAT'S HAPPENING IN THE WORLD.

THE WORLD IS A TERRIBLE PLACE TO START YOUR DAY.

I really try to resist this. But every morning I look. And every morning it makes me sad.

I got this idea because I was always hearing people say, "Make a difference in someone's life." But they never included the word "positive."

I use Rat to get out all my aggressions in life.

It's a wonder Goat still associates with anyone else in the strip. It never ends well.

This really was drawn in a hotel room using a coffee mug. Maybe I should have used the bottom of one of those tiny shampoo bottles instead.

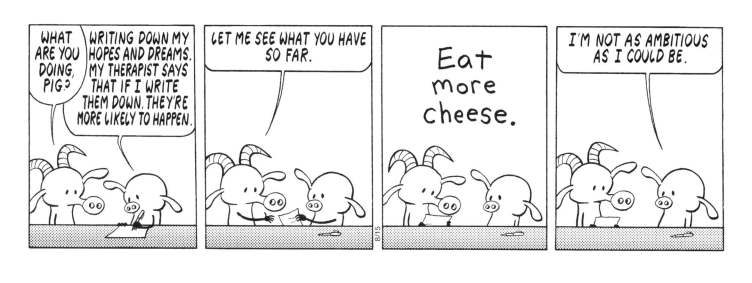

Alas, I did not invent the original expression. It comes from Matthew 7:6.

Panel 1: I'VE CONCLUDED THAT THE FAT ON MY BELLY IS A LOT LIKE THE MOB.

Panel 2: HOW SO? I CAN TRY TO LOSE IT, BUT IT ALWAYS FINDS ME AGAIN.

Panel 3: FAT IS RUTHLESS THAT WAY. MAYBE I'LL TRICK IT BY JOINING A WITNESS PROTECTION PROGRAM.

Panel 4: HOW COME YOU'RE ALWAYS ON TIME FOR EVERYTHING? BECAUSE WHENEVER I AGREE TO MEET SOMEONE, I ALWAYS SHOW UP 15 MINUTES EARLY.

Panel 5: HOW MANY TIMES A DAY WOULD YOU SAY YOU MEET SOMEONE? MAYBE THREE TIMES. TAP TAP TAP

Panel 6: OVER A LIFETIME, THAT'S 20,805 HOURS YOU COULD HAVE SPENT DRINKING BEER.

Panel 7: I DON'T DRINK BEER. YOU SHOULD REALLY START.

I actually did the math on this. It shocked me how many hours it equaled.

Panel 8: HEY, STEPH, WHAT'S THAT STREET THAT THE RUSSIAN RIVER BREWERY IS ON? OH, YEAH... I GO THERE EVERY DAY. IT'S ON....

Panel 9: GOSH, I CAN'T BELIEVE I CAN'T THINK OF IT. GUESS I'M HAVING A BIT OF A MENTAL BLOCK.

Panel 10: YOURS ARE MORE LIKE MENTAL BLOCKADES, WITH GIANT BATTLESHIPS FIRING THEIR GUNS AND PREVENTING ANY WORDS FROM ENTERING YOUR TINY BRAIN HARBOR.

Panel 11: I DON'T NEED YOUR METAPHORS. OH, NO...YOUR WORD BOAT IS SINKING. MAYDAY! MAYDAY!

Russian River is an actual brewery in Santa Rosa, California, the town where I live. They make one of the most famous and well-regarded beers in the world, called Pliny the Younger. People come from all over the world to try it.

The wall in the fourth panel suddenly changed colors. I can't explain that.

81

Eric Van Wagenen is a real person whom I went to school with. Not sure if I still owe him 60 cents.

Jef's line in the last panel was based on a news report that Barack Obama ate exactly seven almonds a night.

I recently went to Savannah, Georgia, with *FoxTrot* cartoonist Bill Amend. It's one of the few places where you can walk around with an open drink of alcohol. One or more of us may have taken advantage of that.

When you have published books, you often get very backhanded compliments. I'm not even sure people are doing it on purpose. For example, someone will say, "You wrote that? I think I read the first few chapters. Didn't finish it, though." I never know whether to say thanks.

This was by far the darkest strip of the year. Even *I* hesitated to run it.

84

The lines in the second and third panels are from an actual poster. The optimism of it always struck me as a bit overblown. So I ruined it for everyone.

I need to put this on a coffee mug.

This is a very uplifting week of strips.

Any similarity to a certain orange-colored president is purely coincidental.

Sometimes at book signings someone will walk up to me and excitedly say we went to grade school together. I often don't remember them. But I act thrilled and hug them anyways.

There are some people who write and let me know that they do not like these pun strips. It only encourages me.

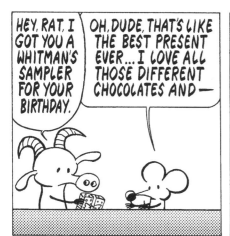

HEY, RAT, I GOT YOU A WHITMAN'S SAMPLER FOR YOUR BIRTHDAY.

OH, DUDE, THAT'S LIKE THE BEST PRESENT EVER... I LOVE ALL THOSE DIFFERENT CHOCOLATES AND—

'I CELEBRATE MYSELF, AND SING MYSELF.'

IT'S A SAMPLER OF WALT WHITMAN POETRY.

AND THEN I BEAT HIM WITH MY BIRTHDAY PRESENT.

I NEVER KNOW WHAT TO DO WHEN I HAVE AN ETHICAL DILEMMA.

AT TIMES LIKE THAT, I THINK IT'S IMPORTANT FOR PEOPLE TO JUST CONSULT THEIR OWN MORAL COMPASS.

MINE POINTS TO, 'DO IT IF IT FEELS GOOD.'

I FORGOT WHO I WAS TALKING TO.

THANKS, LITTLE COMPASS.

I HEAR YOU GOT A JOB AS FEATURES EDITOR OF OUR PAPER.

YEP. AND THE FIRST THING I DID WAS GET RID OF THE BRIDGE COLUMN. WHO IN THE WORLD STILL READS A BRIDGE COLUMN?

OLD PEOPLE ARE FIREBOMBING OUR FRONT PORCH.

PERHAPS I MISCALCULATED.

COOL IT WITH THE MOLOTOV COCKTAILS, GRANDMA!

This was based on something that a features editor told me. He dropped the bridge column and people went nuts.

88

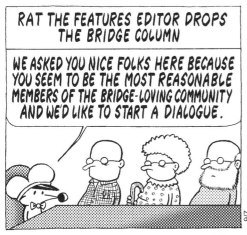

RAT THE FEATURES EDITOR DROPS THE BRIDGE COLUMN

WE ASKED YOU NICE FOLKS HERE BECAUSE YOU SEEM TO BE THE MOST REASONABLE MEMBERS OF THE BRIDGE-LOVING COMMUNITY AND WE'D LIKE TO START A DIALOGUE.

GIVE US BACK OUR BRIDGE COLUMN OR WE'LL SHOOT YOU IN THE KNEE.

BRIDGE-LOVERS CAN BE VERY UNPLEASANT.

This strip drew a truly angry email from a bridge fan extolling the virtues of bridge and telling me to be "more sensitive about what I lampoon." Oh, man. Emails like that will not have the desired effect.

HEY, NEIGHBOR NANCY. HOW'S YOUR WORK GOING?

GOOD. I HELP SET UP YOUTH HOSTELS NOW. SO I RE-DID MY ENTIRE OFFICE SO AS TO FOCUS ONLY ON THAT.

SO YOU HAVE A HOSTEL WORK ENVIRONMENT?

I'LL SHOW YOU HOSTILE.

PASTIS

I regret that this strip wasn't making fun of bridge also.

WHAT ARE YOU WEARING, PIG?

MY PANTS O' DESTINY. WHENEVER I WEAR THEM, I FEEL LIKE I'M ONE STEP CLOSER TO ACHIEVING MY TRUE DESTINY.

DESTINY IS SOMETHING THAT'S INEVITABLE. SOMETHING THAT'S BOUND TO HAPPEN.

I THOUGHT IT WAS THE PANTS.

Should have been about bridge.

Should have been about bridge.

I'm a huge Rolling Stones fan and often write the strip to their *Sticky Fingers* album.

The lions used to be regular characters in the strip. I occasionally get requests to bring them back. Thus, this strip, because I am nothing if not accommodating.

Except to bridge fans.

I will admit right here that in 1987 I had a mullet. And no, I will not post a photo.

Most drivers I knew used to carry a thing called a *Thomas Guide* in their car. It was this bound book with pages and pages of local maps. Without it, you would never know where you were. Man, that feels like a million years ago.

Pet peeve of mine as well. Only I generally don't set fire to the book.

That rule about not swimming until a half hour after you eat was something that every mother
I knew told her kid. Still not sure if there was any validity to it. But I never drowned. So maybe.

I was in Vietnam recently and they're famous for these "water puppet" shows, which is exactly what it sounds like—puppets that emerge out of the water. Sounded kind of cool at first, but then I remembered that it's still a $#%&$@# puppet show. So I went to a bar instead.

I am an organ donor. But not because I wanted to be. My wife turned in the form to the DMV and didn't tell me until later. As I like to say, she is giving me away piece by piece.

My greatest and most effective excuse for getting off the phone is to say, "Sorry if I lose you. I only have one bar." Then I wait 10 seconds and hang up.

Shameless plug: You can find me on Twitter @stephanpastis. And I like followers. Well, not the kind that hide in my bushes.

RAT, THIS IS MY AUNT. SHE HAS THIS GREAT STORY TO TELL.

I'D LIKE TO HEAR IT.

OKAY, DEAR.

I MET THIS BRAVE WOMAN FROM BOULDER, COLORADO, WHO CONSTRUCTS HOUSES.

AND SHE WAS A GREAT, GREAT BOWLER.

HOW GREAT?

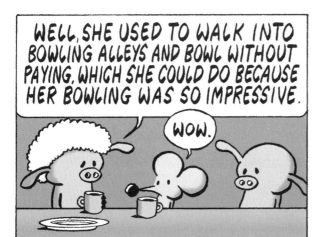

WELL, SHE USED TO WALK INTO BOWLING ALLEYS AND BOWL WITHOUT PAYING, WHICH SHE COULD DO BECAUSE HER BOWLING WAS SO IMPRESSIVE.

WOW.

YEP. AND WHEN SHE WAS DONE, SHE TOLD THE BOWLING ALLEY TO BILL HER FAVORITE BAR FOR THE COST OF THE BOWLING, SINCE THE BAR LOVED TO SPONSOR HER.

YOU MEAN—

9/24

A BOLDER, BOULDER BUILDER BOWLED HER BALL, DEAR. BILLED HER BAR, DEAR.

YOU'RE NOT RIGHT IN THE HEAD.

I've never been to Boulder, but I did ingest an edible in Denver. Then I did a radio interview. Well, someone in my head did. The rest of us just listened.

On the list of things I really want to do, going clubbing is just below getting kicked in the nuts.

I recently went to Raleigh on a book tour. The thing I remember best is eating the chicken and waffles at a place called Beasley's. Holy smokes. One of the best meals I've ever had.

This was another really popular strip.

HI, RAT. I HAVEN'T SEEN YOU IN CHURCH LATELY. I FEAR YOU'VE TURNED FROM THE MORAL TEACHINGS OF THE CHURCH TO THAT OF THE LIMBO DANCE.

THE LIMBO DANCE?

HOW LOW CAN YOU GO?

WE HAVE A VERY SARCASTIC PRIEST.

WHAT ARE YOU DOING, RAT?

I GOT A JOB MAKING WEDDING CAKES. THIS ONE'S FOR A YOUNG COUPLE GETTING MARRIED TOMORROW.

HOP
HOP

THAT CAN'T BE A GOOD SIGN.

For some reason, the guy walking is twice as big as the groom on the cake. So remember, folks, size matters.

WHAT ARE YOU WRITING, RAT?

A GRATITUDE LIST. YOU WRITE DOWN ALL THE THINGS YOU'RE GRATEFUL FOR. IT'S SUPPOSED TO HELP YOU ACHIEVE SOME SORT OF INNER PEACE.

THAT'S WONDERFUL. WHAT DO YOU HAVE SO FAR?

"I'M GRATEFUL THAT I'M NOT GOAT."

NEVER MIND.

IT'S AMAZING HOW MUCH PEACE IT'S GIVEN ME.

I think I've used this same joke twice. I'd be ashamed, if I were capable of feeling shame.

JOJO JUNIOR PACKED FOR COLLEGE.

Well, goodbye, Mom. Goodbye, Dad.

Oh, son, we'll miss you so much.

We love you, son.

BYE. LOVE YOU.

Shoot. Left my favorite pillow in my bedroom.

Hi, I— Home office now. Sold your crap.

THIS IS YOUR 'CONGRATS ON GRADUATING' CARD?

YOU GOTTA SEND THE KID A MESSAGE.

WHY HAVEN'T THEY CHANGED THE LOCKS YET?!

As soon as my son left home, we took the bed out of his room and stuck a couch in there. We stopped short of bolting the doors.

My wife, Staci, is hopelessly practical in terms of the anniversary gifts she wants. So I've never bought her a shoe, but I did once buy her a leaf blower.

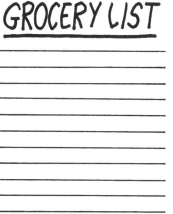

One reader turned this strip into a refrigerator magnet. Not sure if she actually wrote her grocery list on it.

"Screwed" is a word I could not say without difficulty in the first few years of the strip. Newspaper editors would really complain. But now things are a lot more open.

I live in my own personal Ratopia. Everyone loves me there.

10/8

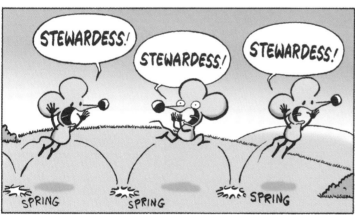

This is a real pet peeve of mine. After all, who decides that we can no longer say the word "stewardess"? And why do we have to listen?

102

This was a pretty popular strip. I think people are a bit worried about our democracy these days.

I had to go to jury duty recently, and after the judge called my name, another potential juror leaned over and said, "Are you the cartoonist?" I was pretty proud. Though admittedly, he never said if that was good or bad.

THANKS FOR COMING OVER TO MY PLACE FOR DINNER, PIGITA. LET ME JUST GET SOME UTENSILS.

WELL, ACTUALLY, PIG, I CAME OVER TO BREAK UP WITH YOU. I FEEL LIKE I CONTRIBUTE A LOT TO OUR RELATIONSHIP AND I'M NOT QUITE SURE WHAT YOU BRING TO THE TABLE.

A FORK AND SPOON.

NO.

WOULD YOU PREFER A SPORK?

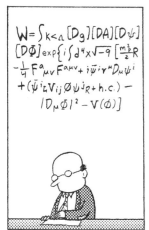

$$W = \int_{k<\Lambda} [Dg][DA][D\psi][D\Phi] \exp\left\{ i \int d^4x \sqrt{-g} \left[\frac{m_p^2}{2}R - \frac{1}{4}F^a{}_{\mu\nu}F^{a\mu\nu} + i\bar{\psi}^i\gamma^\mu D_\mu\psi^i + (\bar{\psi}^i{}_L V_{ij}\Phi\psi^j{}_R + h.c.) - |D_\mu\Phi|^2 - V(\Phi) \right] \right.$$

HEY, PROFESSOR BOB. WHAT DO YOU HAVE THERE?

CORE THEORY. THE PHYSICS EQUATION THAT EXPLAINS ALL OF LIFE.

SCRIBBLE SCRIBBLE SCRIBBLE

Me + BEER = ☺

SIMPLER VERSION.

One time I was wandering around the halls of MIT and saw one of these massive equations on the board of an empty classroom. So I drew Rat right in the middle of it. My apologies if that delayed the cure for cancer.

WENT TO A FANCY DINNER LAST NIGHT. HAD TO GO THROUGH ALL THE USUAL NICETIES.

SEATTLE? CHICAGO? AUSTIN?

WHAT?

THE NICE CITIES.

NO.

WHAT? YOU DON'T LIKE AUSTIN?

I once went to a bar in Austin that bills itself as the smallest bar in Texas. I walked into the tiny bathroom and drew Rat on the wall. At least that bit of graffiti didn't delay the cure for cancer.

 I feel so lonely all the time.

 I do too.

 At least we have social media.

 Yeah, in such a cold world, it's given me real hope.

 Right, like we have a community.

Yeah, instead of always being surrounded by strangers.

Right. Like at the cafe I go to. No one even talks to me.

 Mine too.

 Same as mine.

 Guys... Are we all at the same cafe?

 THIS IS A VERY CONFUSING AGE.

It really is odd how we engage with total strangers online and ignore the people around us. Also, I am writing this commentary in a café where I have not spoken to a single person.

Here's a good rule about cartooning: Never draw bookshelves in the background, because they require you to draw books. Lots and lots of books. And that is time you could have spent drinking at the tiniest bar in Texas.

For some reason, I often draw people who are really leaning to the right, like the guy in the second panel. If he were really standing like that, he would fall backward.

In strips like this, you can really see the influence that *Peanuts* creator Charles Schulz had on me.

Speaking of stupidity, I recently saw a survey where 56 percent of people polled were against teaching Arabic numerals in school. Of course, the numerals we use are Arabic. Stuff like that is a wee bit depressing.

Out for his morning prayer, the saint threw rocks at a dolphin.

OW! OW!

But the saint was attacked by a raven.

'Not so fast,' cried the falcon to the raven, 'I will crush you.'

'ROARRR,' GROWLED THE LION, 'I EAT BIRDS LIKE YOU FOR A SNACK.'

'THINK YOU'RE TOUGH?' YELLED THE VIKING, 'WE HUMANS HAVE SWORDS!'

'YES,' SAID THE COWBOY, 'BUT A COWBOY HAS GUNS!'

10/22

'SURE,' SAID A GIANT...

...BUT I WILL STEP ON YOU ALL.'

WHAT DO YOU MEAN YOU PICKED THE GIANTS TO WIN THE SUPER BOWL?

YEAH, WHAT'S YOUR ANALYSIS?

WAIT... IS A BROWN LIKE A HASH BROWN?

CASINO SPORTS BOOK

BETTING WINDOW

The only time I ever won a sports bet at a casino was when I closed my eyes and let my finger just land on a team.

RAT THE PRESIDENT

SIR, WE'RE HAVING A HARD TIME HIRING A PRESS SECRETARY. NONE OF THE BRIGHT PEOPLE WE'VE INTERVIEWED WANT THE JOB.

FINE. I KNOW A GUY. HE'S NOT VERY INTELLECTUAL, BUT I THINK HE CAN SET THE RIGHT TONE.

KEES LARRY BUTT, JOURNILLEESTS!

I sometimes get complaints that I don't use the crocs enough, so I thought I'd include them in the President Rat storyline.

LARRY, THE PRESIDENTIAL PRESS SECRETARY

SIR, I HAVE A QUESTION ON THE PRESIDENT'S BUDGET.

Okay, but me has joke first.

What difference between journilleest and sad, unemployable loser?

Me not know!

HAHAHAHAHAHAHA

THIS COULD BE A LONG FOUR YEARS.

HEY, I HAVE A JOB! IT JUST DOESN'T PAY MUCH!

There are a lot of pretty heroic journalists out there who deserve a lot more credit and money than they get. So if you can, subscribe to a newspaper and support them.

IT'S GETTING MORE DIFFICULT FOR ME TO LIE.

WHY DO YOU SAY THAT?

BECAUSE I ALWAYS HAVE TO REMEMBER WHAT I SAID TO OTHERS, AND IT'S VERY HARD.

SO WHAT DOES THAT TELL YOU?

THAT I NEED TO IMPROVE MY MEMORY.

NO.

THAT I NEED TO TELL MORE MEMORABLE LIES.

109

LARRY, THE PRESIDENTIAL PRESS SECRETARY

Okay, before we is start, me have say Pressydent Rat no happy wid you coverage.

So today, press conference gonna be in dark.

OKAY, SOMEBODY'S KICKING ME.

HA! You no can prove notheeng!

I think I've said this before, but drawing a lights-out panel is a great way to cut your workload as a cartoonist. I should end all my strips that way.

WHEN THE WORLD ENDS, THERE WILL BE DEBRIS EVERYWHERE. AND THE GROUND WILL BE VERY BUMPY.

SO TO SURVIVE, YOU MUST REST. AND TO REST, YOU MUST SIT. AND TO SIT, YOU MUST BE COMFY.

AND TO BE COMFY, YOU MUST HAVE A LARGE, PADDED BUTT LIKE MINE.

HOW EVOLUTION WORKS
by Pig

I THINK YOUR SCIENCE IS OFF.

LOOK... I'M EVOLVING.

CHIPS

HEY, PIG, WHAT DO YOU THINK OF MY COSTUME? I'M A LAMP.

IT LOOKS GREAT, PIGITA. DOES THE LIGHT WORK?

YEAH. PLUG IT IN AND SEE.

RRR RRR IIING

HANG ON. YOUR MOM'S CALLING.

HI, PIG. CAN I TALK TO PIGITA?

CAN YOU CALL BACK LATER? I'M TRYING TO TURN HER ON.

SHE SOUNDS UPSET.

Hope they don't serve drinks at the costume party. Because she's gonna have trouble holding them.

Coach Knight once famously threw a chair across a basketball court.
Google it. It's pretty funny.

WHAT'S THE MATTER, RAT?

I'M DEPRESSED.

WHY?

BECAUSE I'M RESTLESS. NEVER HAPPY WITH HOW THINGS ARE. ALWAYS WANTING SOMETHING MORE. SOMETHING NEW. SOMETHING GREAT.

I'M CONTENT WITH WHAT LIFE GIVES ME!

SO I PUSHED HIM OFF THE CLIFF.

AND I MET THE NICEST PEOPLE AT THE HOSPITAL!

I am Rat here. Though I wish I were Pig.

WHAT ARE YOU DOING, PIG?

DRESSING UP FOR HALLOWEEN. IT'S THE LAST COSTUME THEY HAD AT THE COSTUME STORE.

DO YOU EVEN KNOW WHAT YOU'RE SUPPOSED TO BE?

OF COURSE I DO.

LUKE, I AM YOUR FATHER.

UMPIRE. NOT DARTH VADER.

ARE UMPIRES AS EVIL?

I HEAR PIG LIKED HIS UMPIRE COSTUME SO MUCH THAT HE BECAME AN ACTUAL BASEBALL UMPIRE.

YEAH.

BUT THAT REQUIRES A GUY WHO CAN BE FIRM.

YOU DON'T THINK HE CAN BE FIRM?

OKAY, IF YOU DON'T LIKE THE CALL, I'LL JUST CHANGE IT.

YOU'LL WHAT?

Now with instant replay, arguments between coaches and umpires are much more rare. That's too bad. It was fun to watch coaches kick dirt on their shoes.

If global warming models are correct, Miami is supposed to be underwater within 80 years.

This is a rare strip in that I end on the joke. No one comments on it after. I'm not sure it really works here, but sometimes I like to experiment.

For me, this really is the way vacation works. First, you try to settle into the rhythm of it. Then, as soon as you do, the vacation is over. So I think all vacations should be around nine months long.

Uber now allows you to tip. I'm gonna credit this strip with that.

I don't know why it happens, but I often get pulled aside by Homeland Security, either for a more thorough search of me or my luggage. Maybe someone there hates puns.

I once visited Babe Ruth's boyhood home in Baltimore, Maryland. That's not very interesting, but neither was his boyhood home, and I couldn't think of anything else to write here.

I watch almost every single Warriors game. I'm a bit of a nutball fan.

This is my favorite of the President Rat strips.

This was a really popular strip. I think the spot color (on just the balloon and the outdoors) made it look a bit different than the normal *Pearls* strip.

Panel 1:
Mouse: EXCUSE ME, SIR, WE'RE LOOKING TO BUY A FRIDGE.

Salesman: WELL, THIS ONE IS OUR BEST MODEL, 22 CUBIC FEET, TOP-OF-THE-LINE WATER DISPENSER, HIGH-EFFICIENCY RATING, STAINLESS STEEL.

Panel 4:
Mouse: AND YET IT CANNOT HOLD A MAGNET.

Salesman: FOR SHAME, SIR, FOR SHAME!

My refrigerator at my studio is almost entirely covered with magnets from places I've traveled to. So I'm a bit biased. Here, see for yourself:

Panel 1:
Mouse: WHAT ARE YOU WRITING, PIG?

Pig: MY THERAPIST SAYS IT'S A GOOD IDEA FOR ME TO WRITE A BUCKET LIST OF ALL THE THINGS I WANT TO DO BEFORE I DIE.

Panel 2:
Mouse: LET ME SEE WHAT YOU HAVE SO FAR.

Panel 3:
Say goodbye.

Panel 4:
Mouse: YOUR STUPIDITY WILL NOT BE MISSED.

Pig: OOH. NO GOODBYE FOR YOU.

A very simple strip, but one that was really well liked. Sometimes the simplest ones are the best.

A comedian named Dick Shawn died while on stage and was lying there for five minutes before the audience realized it was not part of the act.

11/19

It appears Nick has a mouth, but Nancy does not. So at least she won't eat very much.

Goat sits *very* close to the TV. Maybe he's as nearsighted as me.

I recently had a three-hour layover in Hong Kong and thought I'd use the time to leave the airport and go to this really famous dim sum place. But after I left the subway station, I got stuck in some gated, high-rise apartment complex and literally could not find my way out. So that was my trip to Hong Kong.

So "screw you all" is one of those phrases that just could not be said on a newspaper comics page until recently.

The second panel is a great example of how I sometimes draw characters leaning to the right. I think it's easier to see if you turn the strip upside down.

RIP RIP SHRED

WHAT ARE YOU DOING, PIG?

I'M TIRED OF THIS POLITICALLY CORRECT WORLD!

EVERYBODY HAS TO WATCH WHAT THEY SAY! USE THE RIGHT TERMS! THINK THE SAME THINGS! WE ALL HAVE TO BE SO P.C. ALL THE TIME.

SO WHAT ARE YOU DOING AT THIS NEWSSTAND?

I'M MAKING MY VOICE HEARD BY RIPPING UP EVERY SINGLE COPY OF THIS MAGAZINE.

11/26

'P.C. WORLD' IS A MAGAZINE ABOUT PERSONAL COMPUTING.

AND YOU OWE ME A LOT OF THEM.

HEY! 'WINDOWS 10' LOOKS *TERRIFIC*.

I knew at the time I wrote this strip that *PCWorld* had become an online-only magazine, but I needed it to be a print magazine for the joke to work. And thus, it became a print magazine.

Giving everyone a voice has had some serious repercussions. Especially given that there is almost no check on what people can write.

So in the second panel, some big feathers fall to the ground. In the third panel they are gone. You might think that's a mistake by the cartoonist. But no, the truth is that a gardener cleaned up the yard between the second and third panels.

Wrong. My ideas are fully baked. It's the leaning people I can't control.

That number is so big that I had trouble just fitting it into the panel.

125

Lincoln apparently had a great sense of humor. So if he were still president, he'd be a big fan and would probably get a Rat tattoo on his lower back.

Father Gus is the priest at my church. I think he likes it when I put him in the strip. Well, at least he's liked it so far. I'm sure one day I'll cross a line and he'll have Satan take my soul.

Oompa loompas. *Pearls*-speak for testicles. My contribution to the comic strip lexicon.

And yes, my mother is very proud.

Some days the news is so dark you just can't write. Particularly after all of these mass shootings we seem to have so often.

One time in Portland, Oregon, I was picked up by an Uber driver in an SUV that was a mobile karaoke studio filled with bright neon lights and big speakers. I sang an Eminem song. And I was spectacular.

I can spend about an hour in an art museum. After that, profound boredom sets in.

We recently moved my dad out of his house in Phoenix. We took all the stuff he no longer needed, most of which was junk, and put it out on the curb with a "free" sign attached to it. It was amazing how quickly all sorts of people showed up, grabbing stuff like vultures and driving off. Maybe we're all just scavengers.

Some days I'll be on vacation and I'll get back to my hotel room at night and realize I went a whole day without going on the internet. Those are great days.

I have not won any of those awards, but I did recently win the Reuben, the highest award in American cartooning.

Have I mentioned that I recently won the Reuben?

You might not know this, but I recently won the Reuben.

This strip marks the end of my bragging about winning the Reuben.

That's not a badly drawn toilet. It's part of the reason I won the Reuben. Which, if you didn't know, I recently won.

I have almost no interest in the fantasy realm. So if I ever see a wizard or a dragon or a person with pointy ears, I get very bored.

HEY, GOAT, WHAT'S STOCKHOLM SYNDROME? BECAUSE I THINK I HAVE IT.

IT'S WHEN YOU'VE BEEN TAKEN HOSTAGE AND DEVELOP A FEELING OF AFFECTION FOR YOUR CAPTOR.

I SEE. THANKS.

IT'S NOT WHEN YOU SHOP TOO MUCH AT IKEA.

I went to Stockholm once and almost fell out of our second-story apartment. It wasn't really my fault. The whole front wall of it was a huge sliding window that opened to the street, with just a little 1-foot-high section of wall below it. I tripped on the little wall but caught myself on the window frame. And please don't assume I had been drinking. I had. But please don't assume that.

ARE YOU LOOKING FORWARD TO GOING BACK HOME AND SEEING YOUR RELATIVES FOR THE HOLIDAYS?

NO. I ALWAYS FEAR HOME.

WHY IS THAT?

I'M A HOMOPHOBE.

NOT THE WORD YOU'RE LOOKING FOR.

PLEASE DON'T INVALIDATE MY FEELINGS.

I'VE DETERMINED THAT THE AMOUNT OF DEPRESSION IN MY LIFE IS ALWAYS CONSTANT.

HOW SO?

WELL, IF SOMETHING GOOD HAPPENS, I'M HAPPY FOR JUST A BRIEF MOMENT. BUT THEN MY BRAIN QUICKLY FILLS ITSELF WITH SOMETHING ELSE TO BE DEPRESSED ABOUT.

WHAT'S THAT LIKE?

IT'S LIKE THE AUTOMATIC ICE MAKER IN MY REFRIGERATOR. THE TRAY'S NEVER EMPTY FOR LONG.

YOU SOMEHOW MADE ICE DEPRESSING.

I WANT MY COKE WARM!

Since I pretty much only draw coffee mugs and beer glasses, seeing a glass in front of Pig filled with ice cubes is a tipoff that it will be used as part of the joke later.

AND NOW FOR A COMFORTING ADDRESS FROM THE PRESIDENT OF THE UNITED STATES.

OKAY. THINGS ARE BAD.

BUT I AM YOUR PRESIDENT. AND I AM HERE TO IMPROVE YOUR LIVES.

SO HERE IS WHAT I PROPOSE.

I WANT EACH AND EVERY ONE OF YOU TO GO OUT AND BUY A DOG, A GUN, AND A LARGE SUPPLY OF SPAM.

DOG GUN SPAM

THESE THINGS SHOULD CARRY YOU THROUGH THE COMING APOCALYPSE.

SPAM

12/24

BECAUSE IT'S EVERY MAN FOR HIMSELF.

NOT THAT COMFORTING.

FOUR MORE YEARS!! FOUR MORE YEARS!!

I like the fact that this strip ran on Christmas Eve. So while other cartoonists are drawing cute little cartoons with Santa and smiling children, I'm warning of the apocalypse and telling you to stock up on Spam.

And this strip ran on Christmas Day. Because nothing says Christmas like snot on a sneeze guard.

I always hesitate to mention an actual year in the strip, because if the strip is still being read in 20 years, it's going to really date it.

Speaking of getting dated . . . In 2017, the Republicans tried to get rid of Obamacare and replace it with something else. Their slogan was "Repeal and Replace." Thus, this pun, which will only make sense to a few people in the years to come. So my strips, just like milk, apparently have an expiration date.

My son went away to college a few years ago. It's quite the adjustment. So while I didn't actually hide in the closet, I did text him a lot.

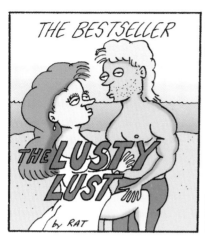

THE BESTSELLER

THE LUSTY LUST

by RAT

"Ron, can you take the kids to soccer practice on Monday?"

"No. That's the night of the homeowners association meeting. Why can't you take them?"

"I'm taking the Honda in for its 100,000 mile service."

"That's due already?"

"Yeah, and the dealership says it's gonna cost around $1200."

12/31

"How are we supposed to afford that?"

THE END

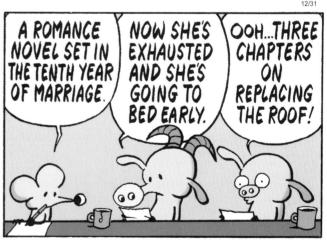

A ROMANCE NOVEL SET IN THE TENTH YEAR OF MARRIAGE.

NOW SHE'S EXHAUSTED AND SHE'S GOING TO BED EARLY.

OOH...THREE CHAPTERS ON REPLACING THE ROOF!

Fun Fact: I recently took my Honda Accord in for its 100,000-mile service. It was very expensive. But the dealership gives you free coffee, so it feels like a good deal.

ALRIGHT, EVERYONE, BEFORE WE RING IN THE NEW YEAR, I THOUGHT IT MIGHT BE A GOOD IDEA TO REFLECT ON THE YEAR WE'VE ALL JUST HAD.

WELL, THAT WAS CATHARTIC.

I could probably run this every single year and it would still be relatable.

I GOT A ROOMBA. I JUST TURN IT ON AND IT VACUUMS ALL MY FLOORS.

THAT'S IT?

WHAT DO YOU MEAN?

MINE DOES MY DISHES.

NOW I FEEL RIPPED OFF.

HEY! GO WRITE MY THANK-YOU NOTES.

My wife recently bought a Roomba. It's disconcerting to go upstairs and see that thing wandering around our rooms. Also, I feel like it's judging me for just sitting there and doing nothing.

WHAT ARE YOU DOING, PIG?

ART. I'M TAKING A PORTRAITURE CLASS. THIS WEEK WERE SUPPOSED TO DRAW VARIOUS SPIRITUAL LEADERS FROM AROUND THE WORLD.

THAT'S NOT WHAT THE DALAI LAMA LOOKS LIKE.

For the most part, I've stopped doing *Family Circus* parodies because I worry that the current generation won't even know who the characters are.

139

LOOKS LIKE THE TEAM IS GONNA PUNT.

WHAT'S A PUNT?

IT'S WHEN THEY GIVE UP BECAUSE THEY'RE TOO FAR AWAY FROM THEIR GOAL AND DON'T WANT TO RISK FAILURE.

IT DOESN'T WORK IN LIFE.

I BROKE A LIGHT.

I LOVE ALL THESE OLD COMEDY TEAMS...LAUREL AND HARDY, ABBOTT AND COSTELLO, THE SMOTHERS BROTHERS.

THAT'S VERY HOMOPHOBIC.

WHAT ARE YOU TALKING ABOUT?

ONE OF THEM ALWAYS HAD TO BE A STRAIGHT MAN.

WE HATE YOU.

In my opinion, Stan Laurel (the skinny one) was the greatest comedian of the 20th century. To me, those silent shorts are the high-water mark of comedy.

HEY, PIG, YOU LOOK A LITTLE DOWN.

YEAH, I'M WORRIED ABOUT THE COUNTRY. ALL THE TRAGEDIES. THE ANGER. THE FIRES. THE SUFFERING. THE DIVISION. THE FLOODS. THE VIOLENCE.

WELL, KEEP ON FLOSSING.

NEVER TRY TO HAVE A DEEP DISCUSSION WITH A DENTIST.

Flossing is time-consuming. Don't do it, kids. And remember, you can always get dentures after your teeth fall out.

140

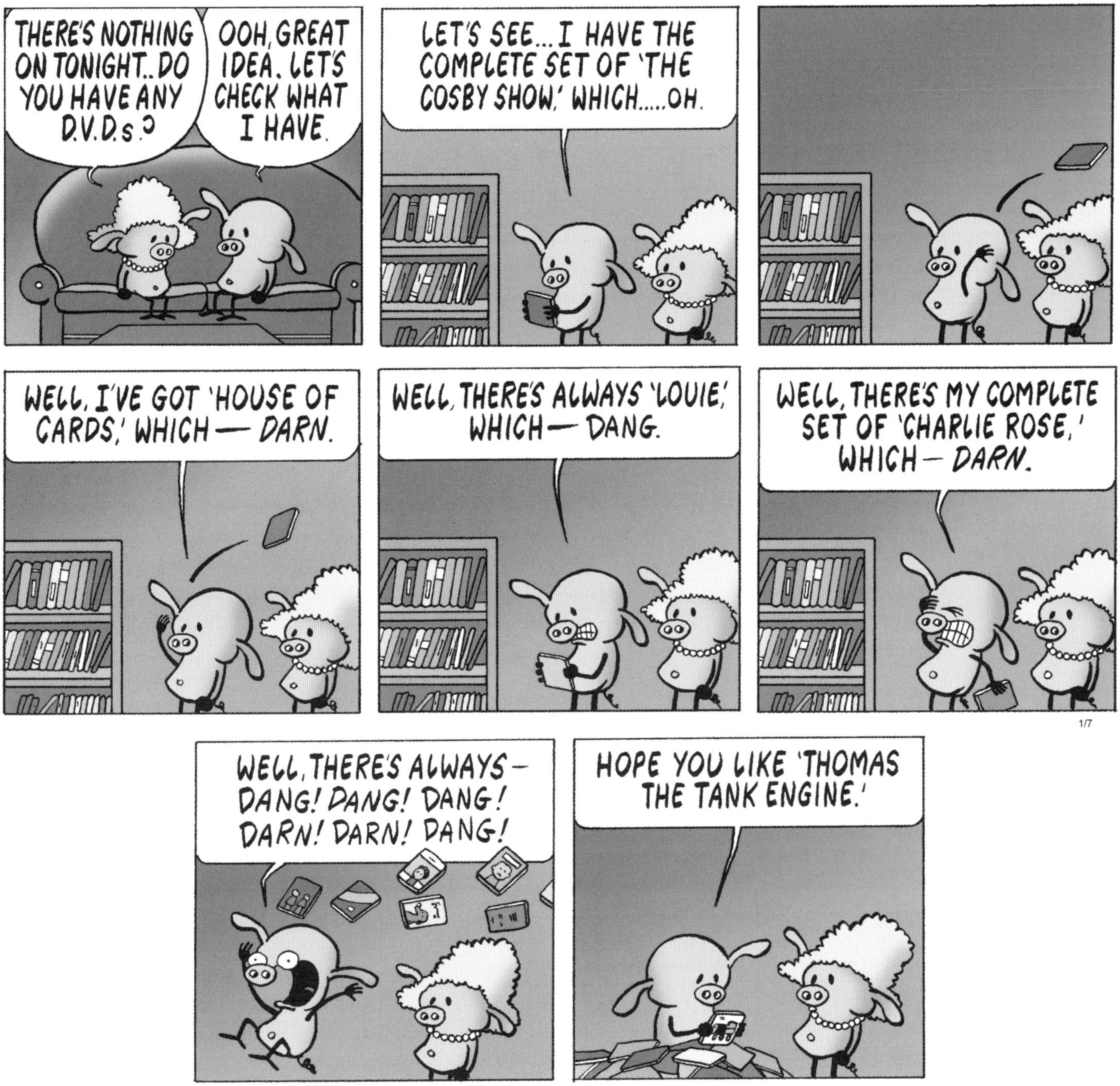

THERE'S NOTHING ON TONIGHT.. DO YOU HAVE ANY D.V.D.s?
OOH, GREAT IDEA. LET'S CHECK WHAT I HAVE.
LET'S SEE... I HAVE THE COMPLETE SET OF 'THE COSBY SHOW,' WHICH.....OH.
WELL, I'VE GOT 'HOUSE OF CARDS,' WHICH — DARN.
WELL, THERE'S ALWAYS 'LOUIE,' WHICH — DANG.
WELL, THERE'S MY COMPLETE SET OF 'CHARLIE ROSE,' WHICH — DARN.
WELL, THERE'S ALWAYS — DANG! DANG! DANG! DARN! DARN! DANG!
HOPE YOU LIKE 'THOMAS THE TANK ENGINE.'

1/7

The guy in the first and the last panel is my friend Lincoln Peirce, the creator of the comic strip *Big Nate*. Lincoln has the very odd habit of keeping binder clips attached to his baseball cap and rubber bands around his wrist. He's a walking Staples superstore.

More of my love for the Warriors sneaking into the strip. I keep hoping that if I do enough strips, they'll invite me into their locker room and hoist me on their shoulders and chant my name.

142

These preppers really do exist. It's a pretty strange and frightening phenomenon.

And for some reason, a lot of these preppers have their shelters in New Zealand. So when the apocalypse hits, they'll be happy and tan and eating kiwis.

Shop at your local bookstore! Truly. You don't want it to go away.
And if they don't have a book you want, they'll order it for you.

I really like this drawing of the Karma Brothers. And no one is leaning to the right.

Surely someone has tried this.

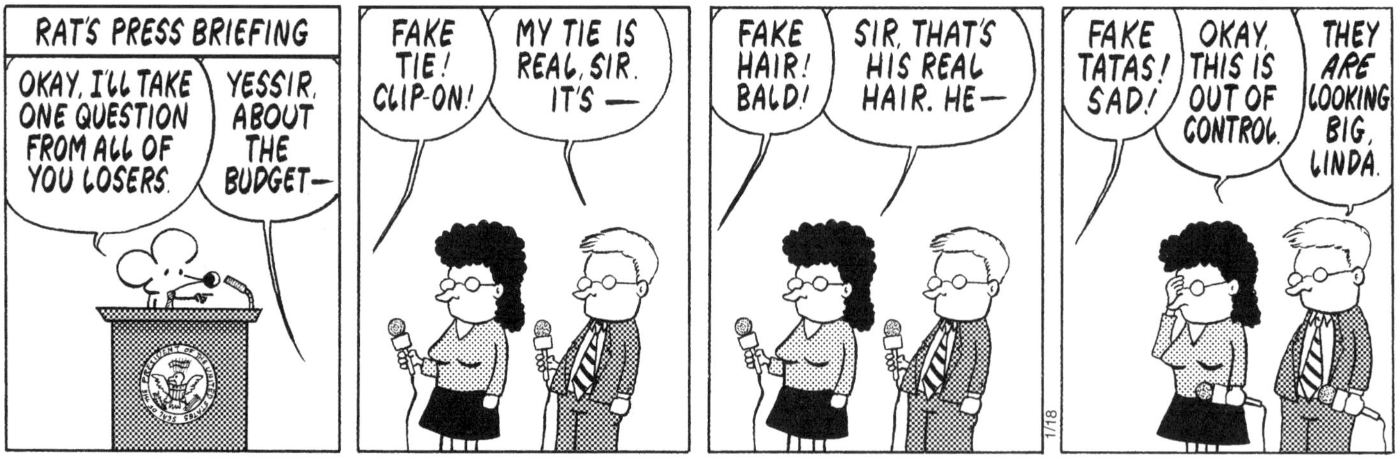
RAT'S PRESS BRIEFING
OKAY, I'LL TAKE ONE QUESTION FROM ALL OF YOU LOSERS.
YESSIR, ABOUT THE BUDGET—
FAKE TIE! CLIP-ON!
MY TIE IS REAL, SIR. IT'S —
FAKE HAIR! BALD!
SIR, THAT'S HIS REAL HAIR. HE—
FAKE TATAS! SAD!
OKAY, THIS IS OUT OF CONTROL.
THEY ARE LOOKING BIG, LINDA.
1/18

In fairness, Linda's tatas do look fake.

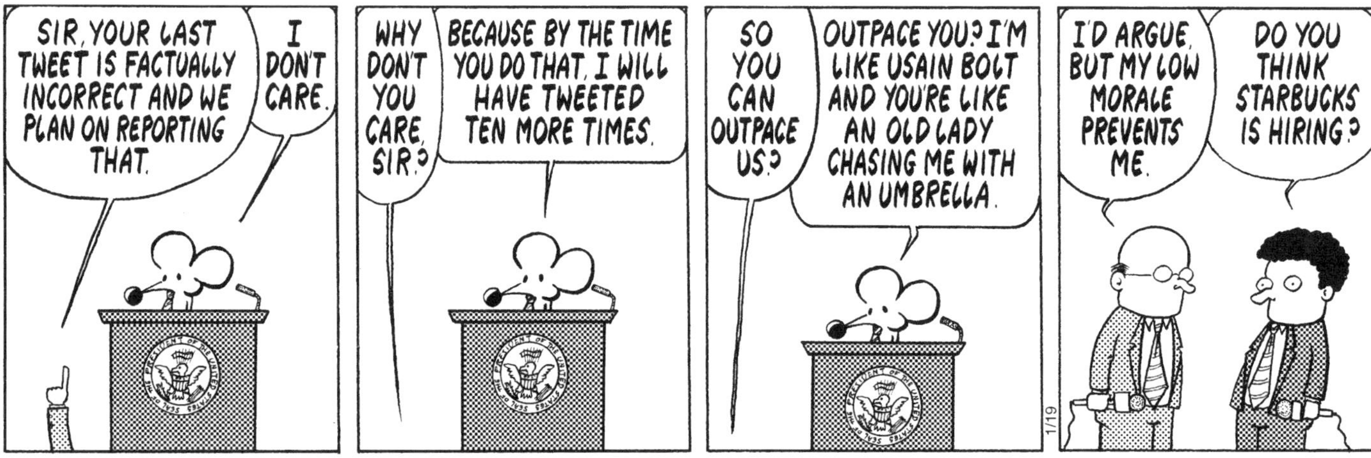
SIR, YOUR LAST TWEET IS FACTUALLY INCORRECT AND WE PLAN ON REPORTING THAT.
I DON'T CARE.
WHY DON'T YOU CARE, SIR?
BECAUSE BY THE TIME YOU DO THAT, I WILL HAVE TWEETED TEN MORE TIMES.
SO YOU CAN OUTPACE US?
OUTPACE YOU? I'M LIKE USAIN BOLT AND YOU'RE LIKE AN OLD LADY CHASING ME WITH AN UMBRELLA.
I'D ARGUE, BUT MY LOW MORALE PREVENTS ME.
DO YOU THINK STARBUCKS IS HIRING?
1/19

I wonder if at some point Twitter and Facebook are going to be held responsible for all the false stories that circulate on those platforms. Every day it seems there is a new story that everyone gets really excited/angry about that turns out to be false or exaggerated. Is it good that anyone can write anything they want?

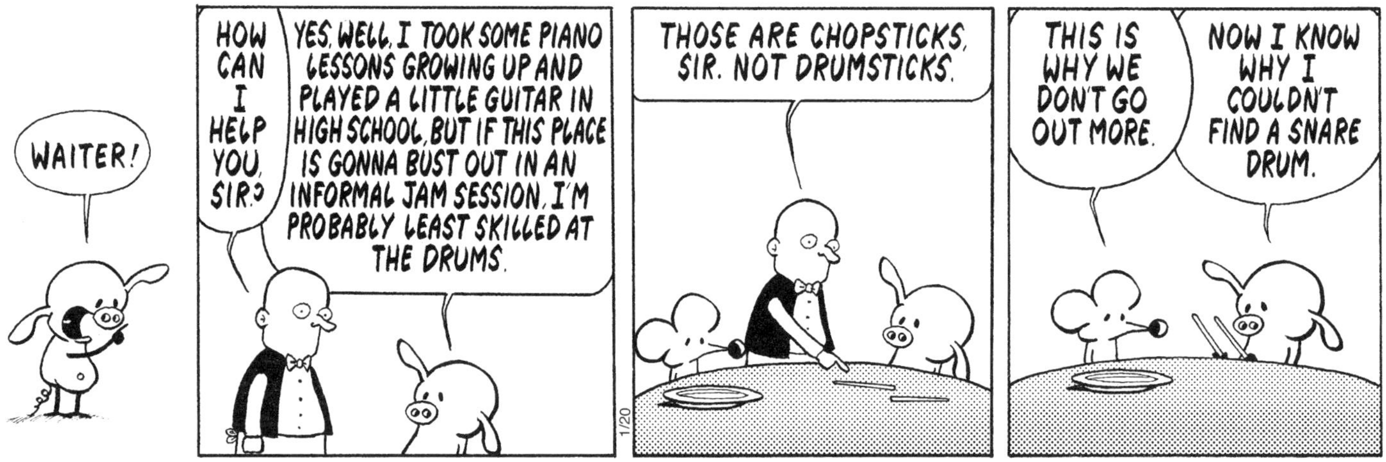
WAITER!
HOW CAN I HELP YOU, SIR?
YES, WELL, I TOOK SOME PIANO LESSONS GROWING UP AND PLAYED A LITTLE GUITAR IN HIGH SCHOOL, BUT IF THIS PLACE IS GONNA BUST OUT IN AN INFORMAL JAM SESSION, I'M PROBABLY LEAST SKILLED AT THE DRUMS.
THOSE ARE CHOPSTICKS, SIR. NOT DRUMSTICKS.
THIS IS WHY WE DON'T GO OUT MORE.
NOW I KNOW WHY I COULDN'T FIND A SNARE DRUM.
1/20

The Six Stages of Marriage

YOU'RE THE GREATEST THING THAT EVER HAPPENED TO ME.

YOU'RE NOT AS GREAT AS I THOUGHT.

YOU NEED TO BE CHANGED.

YOU CAN'T BE CHANGED.

I ACCEPT YOU AS YOU ARE.

1/21

YOU'RE THE GREATEST THING THAT EVER HAPPENED TO ME.

YOU HAVE A SOFT SIDE.

DON'T TELL ANYONE.

This was a really popular strip. Maybe because I don't do these heartfelt strips very often. Always seems to take people by surprise.

147

For those of you who for some reason are *not* alcoholics, a screwdriver is a drink consisting of vodka and orange juice.

Fun Fact: I've been to Arizona a ton of times (my dad lives there) but have never seen the Grand Canyon. You'd think I'd notice such a big hole in the ground.

I don't eat bonbons in bed, but I do eat cookies as I walk around the house. My wife swears I leave crumbs everywhere, so now she makes me put a bowl under it. I drew the line at using a sippy cup.

Holy Timmy the Tortoise. Even **he** is leaning to the right in the first couple panels. I'll blame the heavy shell.

Wassup?

I'm bored.

I'm thinking about punching people.

Not once. But twice.

Biff! Bang!

Right in the bean.

Because I can.

1/28

Okay, little people, that's all I got.

SIR, I THINK PEOPLE EXPECT MORE FROM THE 'STATE OF THE UNION' ADDRESS.

FINE. YOU WRITE IT.

The current president of the United States once bragged that he could shoot people on Fifth Avenue and not get arrested. Rat is only fantasizing about punching them. It's frightening when reality gets ahead of satire.

I think I'd pick the porpoise-driven life. The sea seems like a happier place. Other than everyone eating each other.

I am on Facebook at www.facebook.com/PearlsComic. I post strips, announce new books, and give tour dates.

Confession time. Last week at a restaurant in Berkeley, California, I ordered and ate an entire plate of brussels sprouts. They're not as good as pizza, but they're better than eating paint chips.

So my wife and I recently subscribed to the *New Yorker*. It was great, but I literally couldn't keep up with the long articles, thereby producing the anxiety that Goat goes through here. Overwhelmed, we canceled the subscription.

The insignificance expressed here in regard to the Emmy in no way applies to the Reuben, which is prestigious and has lasting meaning in the cosmic continuum.

152

Tree Stump O' Deep Thought You're Not Usually Capable Of

NO ONE KNOWS WHAT WE'RE DOING HERE.

SOME HAVE FAITH THAT THEY DO, BUT NO ONE *KNOWS*.

SO WE ARE SCARED. WE ARE ALONE. AND WE END. AND WE DON'T KNOW WHERE WE GO.

SO WE CLING TO MONEY FOR COMFORT. AND WE CHASE AWARDS FOR IMMORTALITY. AND WE HIDE IN THE ROUTINE OF OUR DAYS.

BUT THEN THE NIGHT. ALWAYS THE NIGHT.

WHICH, WHEN IT HAS YOU ALONE, WHISPERS THAT MAYBE NONE OF THIS HAS ANY SIGNIFICANCE.

2/4

SO LOVE EVERYONE YOU'RE WITH. BECAUSE COMFORTING EACH OTHER ON THIS JOURNEY WE NEITHER ASKED FOR NOR UNDERSTAND IS THE BEST WE CAN DO.

AND LAUGH AS MUCH AS YOU CAN.

Rarely has a strip I've written had the impact that this one had. It got a huge response, all positive. I think of all the strips I've done, this one comes the closest to expressing my personal view of life.

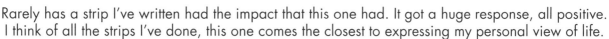

153

GOALS FOR THE WEEK

Accomplish 3 times as much as last week.

Last week: Did nothing.

3 × nothing = nothing

I like experimenting with the rhythm of the comic strip sometimes. And ending on a wordless expression of celebration appealed to me. It's a weird way to close a strip, but I think it works here.

DO YOU EVER GET DEPRESSED WHEN YOU HAVE A BIRTHDAY?

NO. I'M ALWAYS UPBEAT ABOUT TURNING A YEAR OLDER.

WHY IS THAT?

BECAUSE IF I'M EVER SENTENCED TO LIFE FOR MURDER, IT'S ONE LESS YEAR I HAVE TO SPEND IN PRISON.

HOW UPLIFTING.

I SHOULD REALLY WRITE GREETING CARDS.

I really do think the way Rat does here.

I'M GOING TO SOME BIG, FANCY BALL IN A HOTEL.

WHAT KIND OF ATTIRE IS REQUIRED?

I DIDN'T KNOW THERE WAS SUCH A REQUIREMENT.

THERE USUALLY IS.

I FEEL OUT OF PLACE.

This strip is simple and dumb, but I love it. Sometimes simple and dumb is funny.

Pig. Always seeing the bright side.

Seriously. Why the heck do they announce the direction of the wind? What passenger on the plane hears that and says, "Ohhhh, I was wondering about the direction of the wind"?

I should avoid drawing galloping horses. They look more like dogs wearing wigs.

GOODBYE, GOAT. PIG AND I ARE TAKING OFF IN OUR EMERGENCY ESCAPE BALLOON.

HOW COME?

ESCAPE

THE WORLD IS JUST TOO NUTS RIGHT NOW. WE CAN'T TAKE THE ANXIETY.

WHERE ARE YOU GONNA GO?

ESCAPE

DON'T KNOW YET. WE JUST KNOW WE WANT TO GET OUT WHILE WE STILL CAN.

WELL, WHY AREN'T YOU GOING ANYWHERE?

ESCAPE

IT'S A LITTLE CROWDED.

This strip was much too time-consuming to draw. And it wasn't even that funny. Oh well. At least it didn't have any dogs wearing wigs.

MY FRIEND JUST DID ONE OF THOSE D.N.A. TESTS AND FOUND OUT HE'S PART ITALIAN, PART GREEK, SO I TOOK ONE ALSO TO SEE WHAT I AM.

WHAT'S IT SAY?

Bacon.

THESE ARE A REAL RIP-OFF FOR PIGS.

I have always thought I was three-fourths Greek and one-fourth Italian (three grandparents from Greece; one from Italy). But I recently took one of those DNA tests and found out I was half "Middle Eastern," whatever that means. So apparently I am not who I think I am.

DO YOU THINK WE SHOULD LET PEOPLE RUN AROUND NAKED?

NO, IT'S NOT APPROPRIATE.

DO YOU THINK WE SHOULD GIVE DANGEROUS WEAPONS TO KIDS?

NO. OF COURSE NOT.

WHAT IF THEY JUST SHOOT AT US ONE DAY A YEAR?

ARE YOU NUTS?

NOBODY LIKES YOU.

My annoying son, Thomas, often asks me to say the phrase "Irish wristwatch" three times fast. I can't do it. And he knows that. And I really should kick him out of the house.

I just realized those same letters could keep running around and form the word "tinsel." Then the "T" would no longer be silent.

2/18

I once ran for the City Council of Albany, California. I finished last.

RAT THE PRESIDENT

HELLO, SIR. YOU LOOK... DIFFERENT TODAY.

YES, WELL I FIGURED IF I'M GONNA BE KING OF THIS COUNTRY, I MIGHT AS WELL LOOK THE PART.

YOU'RE A PRESIDENT, NOT A KING.

WHAT'S THE DIFFERENCE?

YOU'RE THE ONE WHO CAN'T CHOP OFF HEADS.

THIS WILL BE A LONG FOUR YEARS.

HELLO, SIR, I NOTICE YOU DON'T HAVE THE CROWN TODAY.

YOU SAID I'M NOT A KING, SO I DITCHED IT. BUT I STILL WANT A HAT THAT COMMANDS LOYALTY...RESPECT.

WELL, SIR HOW 'BOUT A NICE FEDORA OR MAYBE EVEN A MODEST TOP HAT OR —

BAD IDEA, SIR.

BLESS YOU, MY IDIOT STAFFER.

That's the hat of the pope. The same fellow who refused to hang out with me when I visited the Vatican.

LOOK AT THAT CHARMING WOMAN OVER THERE. SHE HAS SUCH A WINSOME SMILE.

SORRY, PIG. DO YOU KNOW WHAT THAT WORD MEANS?

YES.

YOU WIN SOME. YOU LOSE SOME.

NO.

TRUE. I NEVER WIN ANY-THING.

This joke is a variation on the "You dim sum, you lose some" strip from a few months prior. Sometimes I write more than one joke on the same theme and then separate the strips by a number of months. So even though they were written together, they don't appear too close to each other.

"Let's tear all our clothes off," yelled Anna.

"Yes!" answered Bob...

"Because all of our clothing has been exposed to bubonic plague."

THAT'S WHERE I THINK IT LOSES SOMETHING.

I really should try writing a romance novel. It would be a spectacular failure. But that still counts as spectacular.

HEY, STEPH, I HEARD A RUMOR THAT YOU'RE SORT OF AN EXPERT ON THE TAPIR AND THAT YOU DO A LOT OF RESEARCH ON THE ANIMAL IN SOUTH AMERICA.

WELL, I USED TO, BUT MY PASSION FOR THE ANIMAL ISN'T QUITE THE SAME THESE DAYS.

IT'S STARTED TO DECLINE?

TAPIR OFF.

I TAPERED HIM OFF.

PIG IS SUCH A BIG FAN OF THE N.B.A. THAT HE GOT A JOB DOING COLOR COMMENTARY.

OH, HE'LL BE GREAT.

THE BALL IS BROWN. THE RIM IS ORANGE. THE SEATS ARE BLUE.

THIS COULD BE A LONG GAME.

This strip is so dumb that I'd prefer you to just look away and never look back.

I once made fun of man buns and got a very funny email strenuously defending them.
Well, the person didn't mean it to be funny. But I found it funny.

I've tried meditating. I can do it for about three seconds.

This would make a good bumper sticker.

Surely, I could slip my head through those widely spaced bars and walk out.

In the last minute of the 2016 NBA Finals, the Golden State Warriors (the team I root for) lost the championship to the Cleveland Cavaliers. To this day, I cannot watch that last minute.

WORK EMAIL

Inbox (325)

To: KJohnsson23482
From: pearlscomic@
Subject: Insurance

Sounds good. Let's
do it for this year.

To: EPack2493@stem
From: pearlscomic@g
Subject: Speaking eng

Sure. Do we want
to meet on the 8th?

To: DSimmons4827@yaho
To: RobertL_Gammbia(
From: pearlscomic@gmail
We might want to circle
Yo: gibbyorem45sff@gma
on that and see who can
Yeah we have enough for
next year, but am worried
To: Joaiohanson@reilly.c
From: pearlscomic@gmail

Inbox (0)

3/4

PING PING PING PING PING PING PING

Inbox (417)

IT WAS THE ONLY SENSIBLE SOLUTION.

I DON'T THINK THAT'S HOW E-MAIL WORKS.

LET THAT BE A LESSON, E-MAIL!

I used to try to answer every email in my inbox, but it was just too time-consuming.
Today, as I look at my Gmail inbox, it shows that I have 375 unread emails.

"Crap" is another word that used to be very hard to say on the newspaper comics page. Now it is pretty much okay, except with some very uptight editors in certain conservative parts of the country. They hate that crap.

Not one of the characters in this strip wears clothes. So how they can have "laundry day" is beyond me.

Panel 1: Dear Guy Who Cut Me Off On The Freeway, You seemed very angry today.

Panel 2: But I'd like you to be happy. So here's a big happy face for you. :)

Panel 3: HE'S HAPPY 'CAUSE HE'S STANDING ON YOUR HEAD.

Panel 4: PLEASE DON'T EDIT MY LETTERS.

When someone honks at me or seems upset with something I've done while driving, I try never to look at them. That way, I can imagine them smiling and holding up "Stephan is great!" signs.

Panel 1: I DON'T KNOW.

Panel 2: NO IDEA.

Panel 3: YOU GOT ME.

Panel 4: WHAT THE @#@# IS HAPPENING TO THE COUNTRY I KNEW?

Another strip influenced by Charles Schulz's *Peanuts*. In this case, by Lucy's psychiatric booth.

Panel 1: PIG'S BEEN WATCHING THOSE HOME IMPROVEMENT SHOWS AND NOW THINKS HE CAN TACKLE ANY HOME FIX-IT JOB. / IS THAT SAFE?

Panel 2: HE'S STARTING OUT SLOW. LIKE RIGHT NOW, HE'S JUST PLUNGING A CLOGGED TOILET. / HAHA... WELL THAT'S SAFE ENOUGH.

Panel 3: CALL 9-1-1. I'M BLIND.

I do this all the time. I do not, however, rifle through their sock drawer.

This was a popular strip. I guess a lot of people have bad knees. Or bad spouses.

I never ran with scissors when I was a kid, but I did accidentally cut open my hand with a steak knife. For reasons I can't explain, I was trying to saw through a box of aspirin at the time. I still have the scar on my left hand.

HAVE YOU EVER NOTICED THAT WHEN YOU GET UP IN THE MORNING, YOU GET ABOUT TWO SECONDS OF BLISS BEFORE YOU REMEMBER ALL OF YOUR PROBLEMS AND ARE SAD AGAIN?

YEAH. WHY?

BECAUSE WHEN IT HAPPENS, GO BACK TO BED, SLEEP ANOTHER EIGHT HOURS AND HAVE YOUR HAPPY TWO SECONDS AGAIN. THEN REPEAT THAT OVER AND OVER UNTIL ONE DAY YOU DIE.

SO THE KEY TO A HAPPY LIFE IS TO SLEEP IT AWAY?

I THOUGHT OF IT FIRST.

AHHHHH

NO FIREARMS ALLOWED ON PREMISES

RULES ARE RULES.

I once set fire to a girl's sweater in a bar in Southern California. Then I put it out and she didn't even say thank you.

RAT HAS NEW NEIGHBORS, LYNN AND JIM.

OH, GREAT. DOES RAT HATE THEM ALREADY?

I ADORE THEM. THEY ARE WONDERFUL PEOPLE. AND I LOOK FORWARD TO A REWARDING FRIENDSHIP FILLED WITH LOVE AND MUTUAL RESPECT.

THEY HOME BREW AND OFFERED HIM AS MUCH BEER AS HE WANTS.

HOME BREWERS ARE GOD'S GIFT TO THE THIRSTY!!

I SEE.

HE ASKED THE POPE TO CANONIZE THEM.

I did a couple fundraisers for a veterans' group in Idaho called Wyakin Warriors. One of the things people bid on was the right to get their name in a *Pearls* strip. This nice couple named Jim and Lynn (who also happen to brew really good beer) had the highest bid and thus they got their names in the strip. I believe that's the only time I've done that.

170

I don't block annoying people on Twitter, because I think they see that you've blocked them and probably derive some satisfaction from that. So instead I mute them and they're none the wiser.

Panel 1: HEY, JEF THE CYCLIST, WHERE WERE YOU THIS MORNING?

Panel 2: CITY COUNCIL. I'M PETITIONING THE CITY TO BETTER ENFORCE ALL THE TRAFFIC LAWS REGARDING CARS. IT'S VERY INFURIATING AND I DEMAND CHANGE.

Panel 3: BUT YOU NEVER STOP FOR STOP SIGNS.

Panel 4: THEN HE BEAT ME WITH GRANOLA BAGS.

Run a strip like this on social media and you are guaranteed to trigger a very heated debate between drivers and cyclists. Sometimes I think I am nothing more than a shit-starter.

Panel 1: WHAT ARE YOU READING? — THIS GREAT BOOK. '1,000 PLACES TO SEE BEFORE YOU DIE.'

Panel 2: INTERESTING. 'CAUSE I'M WRITING A BOOK FOR TEMPORARILY BLIND PEOPLE LISTING ALL THE CLIFFS AND LEDGES THAT POSE A DANGER. — WHAT'S IT CALLED?

Panel 3: '1,000 PLACES TO DIE BEFORE YOU SEE.'

Panel 4: SOME CARTOONISTS TAKE PRIDE IN THEIR WORK. — PRIDE IS OVERRATED.

I actually own the book mentioned in the first panel and have been slowly checking off the places as I travel.

Panel 1: NO, I DON'T KNOW G☆#G ABOUT THAT, BRO. I NEVER READ. I JUST LIKE CHILLING IN FRONT OF THE T.V. FOR HOURS.

Panel 2: PARDON ME, BUT...

Panel 3: IDIOT FREE ZONE

Panel 4: SOME PEOPLE ARE SO INCONSIDERATE.

172

I'VE FINALLY REALIZED THAT MOST OF MY PROBLEMS ARE DUE TO PROCRASTINATION. SO MY RESOLUTION THIS YEAR IS TO CHANGE THAT ONCE AND FOR ALL.

GREAT. STARTING WHEN?

PROBABLY SOON.

THESE THINGS SHOULDN'T BE RUSHED.

GOODBYE, DAD.... OFF TO SCHOOL.

GOODBYE, SON.

PLEASE DON'T GET SHOT. PLEASE COME BACK TO ME ALIVE. PLEASE LET ME HOLD YOU AGAIN. PLEASE.

SCHOOL ENTRANCE

SCHOOL ENTRANCE

SCHOOL ENTRANCE

SCHOOL ENTRANCE

I think this strip caught a lot of people by surprise because they saw Larry in the first panel and assumed it would be silly. If you do strips like this sparingly, they have a much bigger impact.

WHAT ARE YOU DOING, PIG?

I'M IN THE 'SENT EMAIL WHIRLPOOL OF WORRY.'

WHAT'S THAT?

IT'S WHEN YOU SEND AN EMAIL AND DON'T GET AN IMMEDIATE RESPONSE, SO YOU RE-READ AND ANALYZE YOUR EMAIL 6,000 TIMES TO SEE IF YOU POSSIBLY SAID ANYTHING WRONG.

I'LL BE LEADING A NORMAL LIFE IN THE OTHER ROOM.

'THE'... IT WAS THE WAY I SAID 'THE'!

I worry about stuff like this all the time.

173

THE UNFOLDING OF A WELL-PLANNED DAY

6:30 a.m. – Wake up.
7:00 a.m. – Run three miles.
8:00 a.m. – Shower. Get ready.
9:00 a.m. – Write memo for next week's meeting.
10:30 a.m. – Prepare presentation for next week.
12:00 p.m. – Short break for lunch.
12:15 p.m. – 6 p.m. – Do all sales reports by end of day.

7:13 a.m.
Shoot. Overslept.

7:25 a.m.
Not enough time to run three miles. I'll do it tomorrow.

8:02 a.m.
I didn't run, so do I really need to shower?

9:32 a.m.
I can probably write the memo tomorrow.

10:45 a.m.
I'm definitely gonna have to work on the weekend now. Might as well save the presentation 'til then.

12:01 p.m.
I'm hungry, but I have no food. I'll get something at the pub.

3/25

1:37 p.m.
Sure, I'll have another. The whole day's pretty much shot.

11:15 p.m.
I hate myself.

THERE'S ALWAYS TOMORROW.

NO. TOO HUNGOVER.

AT LEAST HE PUT ON HIS WORKOUT SHORTS!!

If the first couple hours of my day are not productive, the whole day spins out of control. So I'm always sure to start working by around 8 a.m. Then I stop somewhere around 7:30 p.m. It sounds like a long day, but I enjoy what I do, so it doesn't feel long.

174

THE MORNING RITUAL

| WAKING | MOMENTARY BLISS THAT A NEW DAY BRINGS | RECOLLECTION OF THE CURRENT STATE OF THE WORLD | RETREAT |

RAT THE PRESIDENT

SIR, WE HAVE A BAD EVENT WE HAVE TO DEAL WITH.

SEND 'EM OUR THOUGHTS AND PRAYERS.

OKAY, WELL, THERE WAS A SECOND EVENT.

THOUGHTS AND PRAYERS.

WELL, THERE WAS ANOTHER UNFORTUNATE—

THOUGHTS AND PRAYERS! THOUGHTS AND PRAYERS! THOUGHTS AND PRAYERS!

AND HERE I THOUGHT WE MIGHT ACTUALLY DO SOMETHING.

TOO TIRED FROM ALL THIS PRAYING.

"Thoughts and prayers" seems to be politician code for "We're not going to actually do anything."

Exercise Goals For The Month:

- Run 5 miles every morning.
- Lift weights 4 times a week.
- Swim every day of month.

- Do one jumping jack while eating cheese.

I LIKE TO INCLUDE ONE I CAN ACHIEVE.

This might be a good time to mention that I won the Reuben, the highest award in American cartooning.

I got this idea from a couple of bars I've seen. One was called "The Library" and another one was called "The Office." I'm sure they were named that so when someone asked a drinker where they've been, they could say "the library" or "the office."

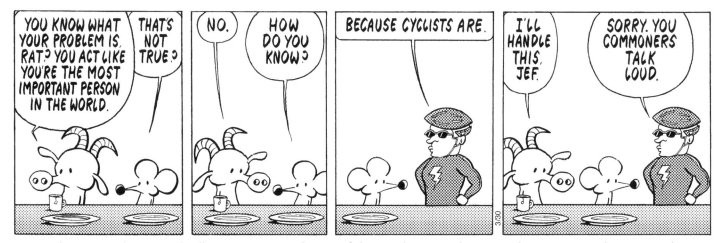

I recently received an email telling me to stop doing Jef the Cyclist strips because they were insulting to cyclists. That inspired me to write two more Jef the Cyclist strips.

176

EXCUSE ME, MR. CONGRESSMAN... I WAS WONDERING IF I COULD TALK TO YOU ABOUT MY BANK.

OF COURSE.

THEY OPENED A FRAUDULENT ACCOUNT IN MY NAME JUST SO THEY COULD CHARGE ME FRAUDULENT FEES.

THAT'S VERY BAD.

NOW I KNOW BANKS GIVE YOU A LOT OF MONEY AND WINE AND DINE YOU, BUT I HAVE VERY MODEST MEANS.

THAT DOESN'T MATTER... I REPRESENT YOU.

OH, WOW, SO YOU'LL DO SOMETHING ABOUT IT?

YOU **BET** I WILL. I'LL PUT THAT C.E.O. IN JAIL JUST LIKE I WOULD ANYONE WHO COMMITTED THAT KIND OF FRAUD AND I'LL GET ALL YOUR MONEY BACK FOR YOU!

OH MY GOD, THANK YOU, THANK YOU. WHEN DO YOU THINK YOU CAN DO ALL THAT?

4/1

WELL, LET ME JUST CHECK MY CALENDAR AND...

APRIL FOOLS!!

APRIL 1

SHOULD I LAUGH OR CRY?

MOSTLY CRY.

HAHAHA... HE BELIEVED IN DEMOCRACY!

I don't do a lot of April Fools' strips, but this one was irresistible. It was based on a story in the news at the time about a large bank that opened fake accounts in people's names in order to charge them fraudulent fees.

This drew a complaint from someone about my making a "fatphobia joke combined with ridiculing disabilities."

Jerry Scott, the cartoonist behind *Zits* and *Baby Blues*, paints really great horses and cows. He's a pretty incredible painter.

I think cyclists would be perceived better if they would just avoid wearing their spandex in cafés. No one wants to see your oompa loompas while they're sipping a latte.

A newspaper once thought I snuck the F-word into a *Pearls* strip. But I really didn't. It was just the result of that particular paper compressing the strip vertically and making a bunch of jumbled text look like it said something it didn't. The story even made the nightly news.

HEY, YOU'RE FINALLY CLEANING OUT THE GARAGE.

YEAH. TRYING TO DECIDE IF I SHOULD KEEP THIS SCUBA GEAR.

YOU HAVEN'T GONE SCUBA DIVING IN YEARS.

YEAH, BUT WHAT IF I NEED IT ONE DAY?

PLEASE. AND WHADDYA NEED THIS RACCOON TRAP FOR? IT'S BEEN YEARS SINCE WE HAD TO TRAP ANY.

TRUE. AND THESE KEYS.

YEAH. WHAT ARE YOU KEEPING THOSE FOR?

I DUNNO. THIS ONE WAS TO GET INTO NEIGHBOR BOB'S BACKYARD WHEN WE TOOK CARE OF HIS POOL. BUT YEAH, YOU'RE RIGHT....

SEE? IT FEELS GOOD.

YEAH. YOU GET SO BURDENED IN LIFE BY ALL THE STUFF YOU KEEP.

CITY DUMP

4/8

GUYS! COME QUICK! NEIGHBOR BOB'S TRAPPED AT THE BOTTOM OF HIS POOL, BUT HIS GATE'S LOCKED AND IT'S GUARDED BY AN ANGRY RACCOON!!!

WELL, BOB HAS BAD TIMING.

ALWAYS..KEEP...EVERYTHING!!

CITY DUMP

I wanted to teach my daughter, Julia, how to use Adobe Photoshop, so I showed her a few things, and this is the first strip she colored. Sadly, it was better than mine, so I fired her.

180

SOFT SHOULDER

THERE, THERE, SWEETHEART...THE WORLD'S A TOUGH PLACE RIGHT NOW, BUT EVERYTHING WILL BE OKAY.

WE NEED MORE OF THOSE.

This should be available every few miles.

HEY, PIG, HOW WAS YOUR DINNER WITH PIGITA LAST NIGHT?

GREAT. I CONSUME A LOT LAST NIGHT.

YOU KNOW, PIG, I'VE EXPLAINED THIS TO YOU. WHEN THE ACTION IS IN THE PAST, YOU NEED TO USE THE PAST TENSE OF THE VERB.

I CONSUMMATED A LOT LAST NIGHT.

MAYBE GO WITH THE PRESENT TENSE.

SHE CONSUMMATED A LOT, TOO.

STEPHAN?

YEAH?

DID YOU FINISH YOUR PAPER ON MACBETH?

I DIDN'T KNOW IT WAS DUE.

DIDN'T KNOW IT WAS DUE?... WELL THEN YOU'RE NOT PASSING THIS CLASS, AND YOU'RE GOING TO HAVE TO DO HIGH SCHOOL ALL OVER AGAIN.

ACT I...
ACT II...
PLOT
THEME!

HAPPENS EVERY TIME I TAKE HIM TO SEE A SHAKESPEARE PLAY.

SOME GUYS JUST DON'T APPRECIATE CULTURE.

NO...PLEASE... HELP.

I have this nightmare. I also have one where the law firm I used to work for discovers that I haven't been turning in time sheets for the last 19 years.

181

My wife's Roomba has had a profound effect on me.

No one with "I can't stop $&#@*$# up syndrome" complained about this strip.

Being allowed to say "sucks," "screwed," and "crap" has really opened things up for me. It's like giving Mozart more notes. And yeah, I just compared my using the word "crap" to one of Mozart's compositions.

I've been to President Truman's library in Missouri, as well as to the libraries of Kennedy, Johnson, Nixon, Carter, and Reagan. I'm a bit of a presidential library junkie.

I don't think I've sent a thank-you note since high school. I should just copy and paste the third panel.

I think I blew this strip by making Rat's line in the last panel too long. By that point in the strip, the joke's already done and you have to be quick. I can really only see mistakes like this when I look at the strip many months later.

I do this when I go to get hamburgers and fries for me and my son. Other than that, I'm a stellar father.

I don't fear cows, but I do fear the electric fences they sometimes put around them. I've grabbed those stupid things not once, but twice. I found it shocking.

HEY, PIG, WHAT ARE YOU DOING?

THIS IS MY DOCTOR. HE'S TRYING TO LEARN WHAT NOUNS AND VERBS ARE.

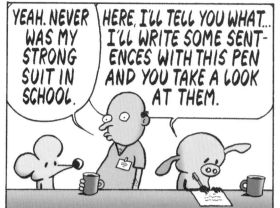

YEAH. NEVER WAS MY STRONG SUIT IN SCHOOL.

HERE, I'LL TELL YOU WHAT... I'LL WRITE SOME SENTENCES WITH THIS PEN AND YOU TAKE A LOOK AT THEM.

The ewe ate grass. The man was angry. The dog barked.

OKAY, SO NOW WHAT DO I DO?

TAKE THIS RED CRAYON AND IN EACH OF THE SENTENCES, I WANT YOU TO CIRCLE ALL OF THE NOUNS.

WHAT'S WRONG?

I'M CONFUSED ALREADY.

I MEAN, FIRST OFF, DO YOU WANT ME TO USE THE PEN OR THE CRAYON ON ALL THESE? AND WHAT TYPE OF WORD IS 'EWE'?

'EWE' AIN'T NOTHING BUT A NOUN, DOC. CRAYON ALL THE TIME.

DON'T BE CRUEL.

This is based on the Elvis lyric from the song "Hound Dog." And crying is what people do around Elvis's grave at Graceland, a place I've now been to three times. They grieve for him like he was a quasi-religious figure. It's pretty incredible to see.

Some cultures believe it is good luck if a bird flies into your house, but others think it is bad. I don't know which one of them is right, so I just try to keep all birds out of my house.

Not one person is happy to discover coconut in the middle of their chocolate candy. Not one. The chocolate people just do it because it makes them laugh.

In lieu of this, you can just buy the "NO SOLICITING" sign I have that ends with a stupid, unnecessary "thank you."

This "tiny house" movement is a real thing. They're under 400 square feet, or roughly the size of a large New York apartment.

4/29

I do have a lot of people ask me why the crocs aren't in the strip as much anymore, so I thought I'd give them a reason.

I was recently in Saigon, Vietnam, running on a treadmill in my hotel. Suddenly, the whole thing momentarily stopped, and I almost went through the mirrored wall. Hey, when it's your time, it's your time.

This was based on my real life. I was without it for just a few hours, but it's crazy how much even that can disrupt your life.

None of the fine people at Pledge offered me any free Pledge for this fine product placement. That's okay.
I don't dust anyways.

My best friend Emilio would not tell me the mantra he received at his meditation class. He's a big, dumb idiot,
and I hope he never achieves inner peace.

Speaking of cheese, I was recently in Oregon, where I walked into a deli to buy cheese. Well, I was a little bit stoned (hey, legal there!), and when the woman asked me what kind of cheese I wanted, I couldn't believe she was asking me that. Because in my mind, there was only one kind of cheese and she was obviously harassing me. So I just kept answering, "Cheese. You know, the kind that's just cheese."

 **Achieving your dreams is the key to a happy life. So write down a dream and go for it. And when you achieve it, CELEBRATE!**

 Be fat and lazy.

Another experiment in ending on a wordless panel. There's something about it I like. Maybe just the simplicity.

 WHAT ARE YOU DOING, RAT? / TRYING TO WRITE A BOOK, BUT WRITING IS HARD.

 WELL, THEY SAY THE KEY IS TO JUST EXPRESS WHAT'S INSIDE YOU.

 Anger. Anger. Anger. Anger. Anger. Anger. Anger. Anger. Anger. Anger. Anger. Anger. Anger. Anger. Anger.

I'M NOT SURE IT'S VERY COMMERCIAL.

 HEY, MOM, DAD SAYS HE'S GONNA FLY ALL OVER THE WORLD. / JUNIOR, YOUR FATHER DOESN'T HAVE A JOB. HE CAN HARDLY AFFORD TO FLY ANYWHERE.

 HE SAYS HE CAN DO IT FOR FREE. / AND HOW'S HE GONNA DO THAT?

 Emoshunal Support Crocydile Avaylable. Prob no keel u

This was based on a story in the news that someone had tried to bring a peacock on board a plane, claiming it was their emotional support peacock.

HEY, RAT, WHY ARE YOU LATE TODAY?

HAD TO GO TO A MEMORIAL FOR ONE OF OUR NEIGHBORS. IT WENT A LOT LONGER THAN IT SHOULD HAVE BECAUSE HIS WIDOW INVITED ANYONE WHO WANTED TO SAY SOMETHING TO COME UP AND SPEAK.

DID YOU GET UP AND SAY ANYTHING?

I DID.

YOU'RE ALL RESPONSIBLE FOR MY EXPIRED PARKING METER.

I recently went to a memorial where people were invited to come up and speak. At first, people were hesitant. But then all these people started walking up, some with very tangential connections to the deceased. After an hour or so of this, I wanted to start tackling them before they could get to the podium.

CAN'T COPE.

SO GONNA FIND A NICE QUIET PLACE IN THE SKY.

SO GONNA FIND A NICE QUIET PLACE IN THE SKY.

THAT SEEMS LIKE CHEATING.

HEY, GOAT, DID JIMMY THE TOWN BARBER RETIRE?

YEAH. HE GOT REPLACED BY A NEW GUY, BUT I'M AFRAID HE DOESN'T HAVE MUCH EXPERIENCE... WHY?

NO REASON.

This is one of those strips that just resulted from a sketch I did in my notebook.

A very popular strip. I made sure to run it on Mother's Day.

I mention Fritos quite a bit. HEY, FRITOS PEOPLE—SEND ME BOXES OF FREE FRITOS OR I WILL START SHILLING FOR CHEESE PUFFS.

This strip originated from an indie bookseller telling me that a customer did this to her. She helped them find the book they wanted and then they went on their phone and bought it on Amazon.

196

Not that far from reality these days.

I once got to work with Mark Mothersbaugh, the lead singer of Devo. He did the music for a *Peanuts* TV show I cowrote called *Happiness Is a Warm Blanket, Charlie Brown*.

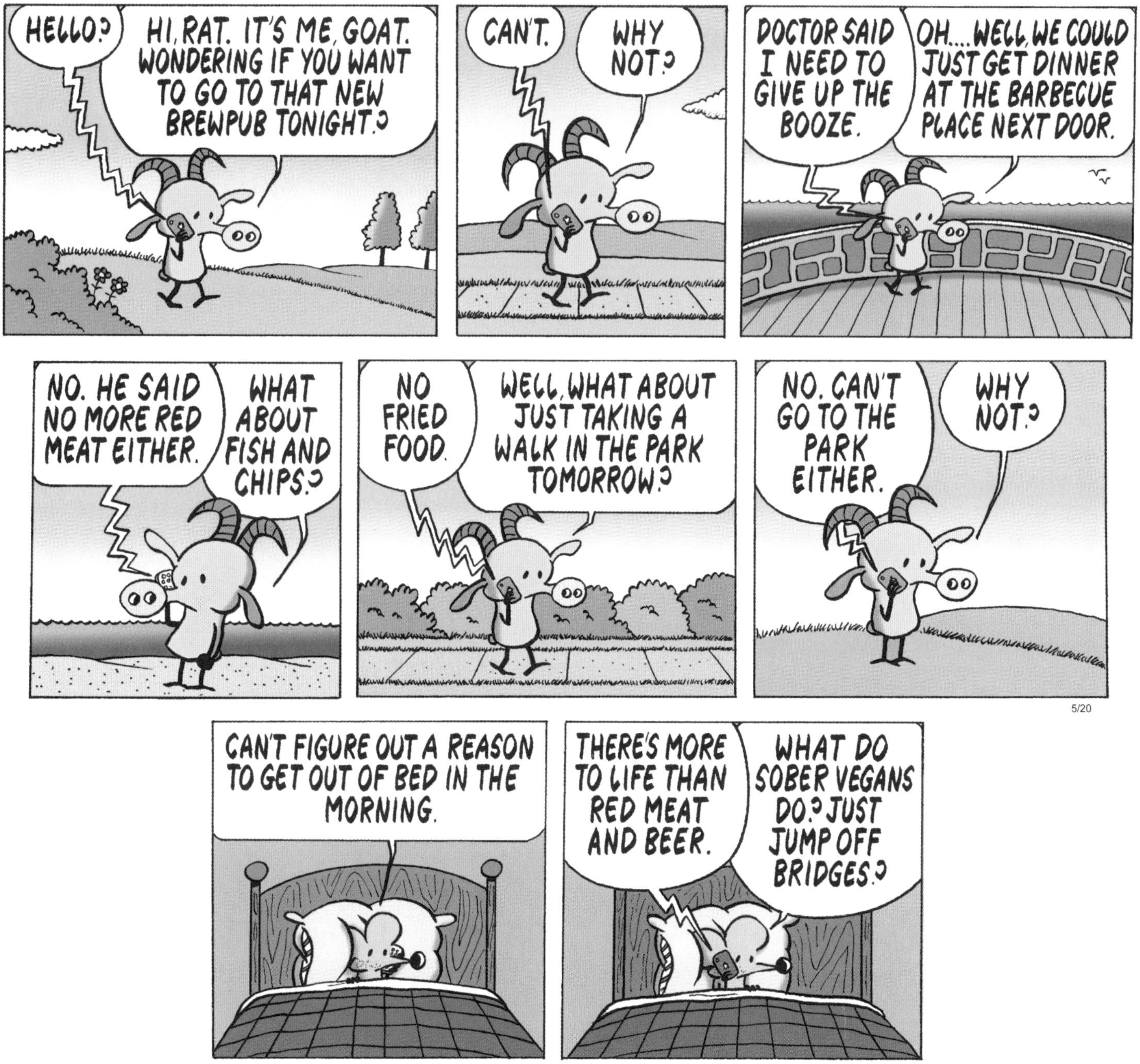
HELLO?
HI, RAT. IT'S ME, GOAT. WONDERING IF YOU WANT TO GO TO THAT NEW BREWPUB TONIGHT?
CAN'T.
WHY NOT?
DOCTOR SAID I NEED TO GIVE UP THE BOOZE.
OH....WELL, WE COULD JUST GET DINNER AT THE BARBECUE PLACE NEXT DOOR.
NO. HE SAID NO MORE RED MEAT EITHER.
WHAT ABOUT FISH AND CHIPS?
NO FRIED FOOD.
WELL, WHAT ABOUT JUST TAKING A WALK IN THE PARK TOMORROW?
NO. CAN'T GO TO THE PARK EITHER.
WHY NOT?
5/20
CAN'T FIGURE OUT A REASON TO GET OUT OF BED IN THE MORNING.
THERE'S MORE TO LIFE THAN RED MEAT AND BEER.
WHAT DO SOBER VEGANS DO? JUST JUMP OFF BRIDGES?

 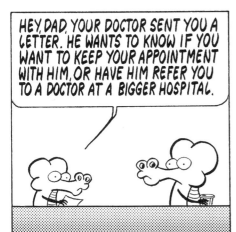   

Larry's unique way of talking gives me opportunities for jokes that I don't have with other characters.

I wanted to make the "No One Cares" Duck a regular character, but I already have a duck character. Maybe I'll introduce the "No One Cares" Loon.

Speaking of kids' heads, one time these friends of ours came over to our house and lifted our one-year-old son, Thomas, high into the air. But they lifted him too high. And WHAM, he hit his head on the ceiling.

Again, never mind the fact that Pig doesn't even wear clothes.

CHEESE TASTES AWESOME.

PEOPLE SHOULDN'T DRIVE SLOW IN THE FAST LANE.

CHOCOLATE MAKES EVERYTHING BETTER.

IT'S ANNOYING WHEN THE NEIGHBOR'S DOG BARKS ALL DAY.

A WARM, COZY BED FEELS GOOD ON A COLD, WINTER DAY.

DISCO NEVER SHOULD HAVE HAPPENED.

BEER... BEER BEER!

5/27

PRINTER INK IS TOO EXPENSIVE.

SOME MEN SHOULDN'T WEAR SPEEDOS.

THINGS A DIVIDED COUNTRY CAN STILL AGREE ON

I agree with everything but the third panel. Never been a big chocolate fan.
PARTICULARLY WHEN SOMEONE HIDES COCONUT IN THE MIDDLE.

I have to admit, people who can regularly rise before dawn seem to get a lot more done. It's supposed to be very quiet and easy to concentrate at that time of day. I wouldn't know because I've never done it. Unless you count being up in Miami at 5 a.m. because you've been drinking all night. That wasn't that productive.

This happened to me at a post office in Santa Rosa, California. It was almost too cruel to be believed.

Pig's expression in the third panel really has to carry the joke, which is his realization that he has said too much. Gee, my strip would be so much better if I could always explain the joke in text just below the comic strip.

I wonder if anyone has ever tried to calculate the total value of all the office supplies stolen every year. It has to be in the millions.

This would be a very useful feature.

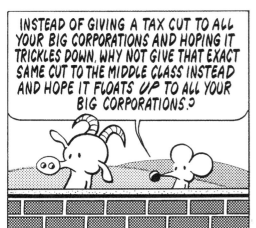

INSTEAD OF GIVING A TAX CUT TO ALL YOUR BIG CORPORATIONS AND HOPING IT TRICKLES DOWN, WHY NOT GIVE THAT EXACT SAME CUT TO THE MIDDLE CLASS INSTEAD AND HOPE IT FLOATS *UP* TO ALL YOUR BIG CORPORATIONS?

WE'LL CALL IT 'UP YOURS' ECONOMICS.

I'LL WRITE MY SENATOR.

YEAH...TELL CONGRESS, 'UP YOURS.'

I drew this strip around the time that Congress was enacting this tax cut and I didn't want to wait six months for people to see it (that's roughly how far I am ahead of deadline). So I did something unusual that I hadn't done before or since—I put it online the same day I drew it. And since the tax topic was hot at that moment, it received a very large response. It made me really envy webcomics that can get this instant reaction every day.

Dear life as I know it...

You changed.

Please be normal again.

WHERE DOES ONE SEND THESE?

HELLO?

HELLO, PIG. IT'S YOUR MOTHER. I'M WORRIED ABOUT YOU. WHAT'S YOUR PLAN FOR LIFE?

GO TO A GOOD SCHOOL. WORK HARD. SUCCEED.

AND WHAT'S YOUR PLAN B?

FAIL.

SHE DIDN'T LIKE MY PLAN B.

This came from a conversation I had with my mom when I told her I was quitting my law firm job to draw a comic strip. She asked me what my Plan B was if the cartooning thing didn't work out. I told her I didn't have one.

This is me and my son. I text him and he doesn't text back. I threatened to cut off his food, but he didn't respond to that text either.

Drinking a beer on the back porch is often the best option in life.

After this ran, some cyclist complained that suggesting they beat each other with sacks of granola was not funny. Feedback like that only encourages me.

WHAT ARE YOU DOING, RAT?

JUST HUNG THIS PAINTING OF AN ELEPHANT. TOOK A WHILE TO GET IT CENTERED AND LEVEL. HOW DO YOU THINK I DID?

IT'S WELL HUNG.

I THINK YOU KNOW WHY I'M HERE.

BECAUSE IT'S NOT STRAIGHT?

IS IT THE ELEPHANT IN THE ROOM?

COMIC STRIP CENSOR

This was really pushing the proverbial envelope, at least for a newspaper comic strip. Surprisingly, I didn't hear of any editor complaints.

I HAVE A NEW MOTTO THAT GUIDES ME IN LIFE: BE THE CHANGE YOU WANT TO SEE IN THE WORLD.

I LOVE THAT.

THAT SURPRISES ME TO HEAR YOU SAY THAT. SO YOU AGREE YOU NEED TO BE THE CHANGE?

NO, YOU. YOU BE THE CHANGE. I'LL BE THE SAME SELFISH @## I'VE ALWAYS BEEN.

I THINK YOU'RE MIS-USING THE MOTTO.

BUT YEAH, EVERYONE ELSE SHOULD CHANGE.

HIYA, DAD, I'M HOME FOR SEMESTER BREAK. WHAT ARE YOU DOING?

Me trying put togedder stoopid bookcase.

IS IT HARD?

Yeah, becuss stoopid P.C. police say direckshuns got be in all sorts of foreign languages ME NO CAN READ!

THAT PART'S IN ENGLISH.

When stoopid son go back to school?

I like leading people to believe I'm about to comment on something political (like people not speaking English in this country) and then turning it around to make a silly joke about Larry's stupidity. Confounding expectations is the name of the game in comic strips.

The publisher of this book you are holding also publishes a lot of coloring books for adults, and they are very proud of that fact. So if this particular strip has been crossed out with thick black pen, you know why.

Fun Fact: I drink a lot of apple cinnamon tea when I write. And as I told you earlier, these "fun facts" are almost never fun. They're not even moderately interesting. But they are facts. At least when they're not lies.

Clearly, 2017 and 2018 were the years that the news really started to get to me.
When that happens, I go and sit in a forest near our house. But the other day
I found a scorpion there. So maybe I'll just go to a bar.

HELLO?

HI, PIG, IT'S YOUR MOM. I HATE TO BUG YOU, BUT I'M WONDERING... DO YOU HAVE A PLAN FOR YOUR LIFE?

YES, I DO.

GREAT. I'D LIKE TO HEAR IT.

EAT SO MUCH CHEESE I SLIP INTO A HAPPINESS COMA.

SHE WAS THINKING LAW SCHOOL.

HEY, STEPH, YOU SHOULD START SIGNING YOUR STRIPS. I NOTICE ALL THE OTHER CARTOONISTS DO IT.

YEAH, I NEVER REALLY SAW A REASON TO DO IT.

BECAUSE IT SHOWS WHO DID THE WORK. YOU SHOULD BE REALLY PROUD OF THAT.

OKAY. I'LL SIGN IT IN THE THIRD PANEL.

THERE. THAT'S GREAT.

YEAH, IT DOES FEEL GOOD TO TAKE PRIDE IN MY WORK LIKE THAT.

NOW I CAN FORGE HIS CHECKS.

After I did this strip, I thought, "Hey, maybe people *will* use it to forge my checks." So I used a different signature.

HEY, GOAT, WHEN WE DIE, DO WE DISAPPEAR COMPLETELY?

WELL, PIG, THE LAW OF CONSERVATION OF MASS SAYS NO. THE ATOMS THAT COMPOSE US JUST SCATTER AND GET USED FOR OTHER THINGS.

SO WE'RE NOT DEAD, WE'RE JUST DISORGANIZED.

WELL...

SO I BECOME LIKE THE TOP OF MY DESK.

The desk where I work is actually really organized. Everything has to be in its right place or I can't work. Also, if the tissue is sticking out of the tissue box (as it normally is), I have to tuck it into the box before I can start working.

211

If I remember right, I think the Flaming Lips took notice of this strip. But what do I know? I get distracted by Kleenex.

Last week I went to *The Simpsons* writing room on the Fox lot in Century City, California. I know one of the longtime writers of the show. Every time I go there, it's like visiting hallowed ground.

212

6/24

It's crazy to me that so much of the country would rather their party "win" than for progress to be made. Seems to me like we are all in the same battered boat and we sink or swim together. But really, don't listen to me. I fear Kleenex.

213

When I was a kid, *Bugs Bunny* cartoons had a huge effect on my sense of humor. I can see it in strips like this.

As I understand it, a lot of great writers like Ernest Hemingway and Jack London reserved their mornings for writing and only started drinking after they were done. Much more productive than the other way around.

Today I will waste seven hours. Then I will be productive for just one hour.

Then I'll hate everything I did.

Then I'll think I'm a joke.

Then I will take out all my frustration on the person closest to me.

'HOW TO BE A WRITER,' CHAPTER ONE.

HOW APPEALING.

WHEN DOES THE DRINKING START?

I did a lot more strips about writing in 2017 and 2018, probably because I was spending so much of my time writing the *Timmy Failure* movie.

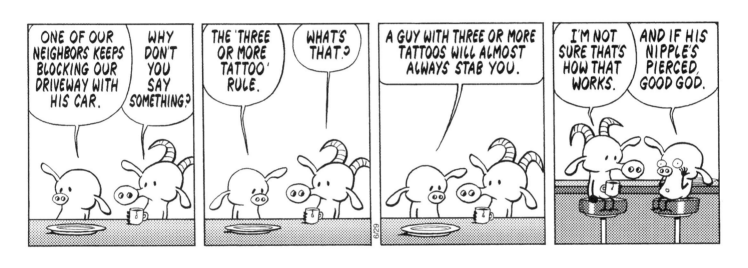

Why is "little people" a better term than "midget"? Who decides these things?

HEY, GOAT, THESE ARE MY AUNTS. THEY'RE RAISING CASH FOR A CORN FLAKE.

A CORN FLAKE?

IT'S *THE* FLAKE OF THE UNITED STATES. IT WAS ON THE TABLE WHEN JEFFERSON SIGNED THE DECLARATION OF INDEPENDENCE.

AND YOU'RE RAISING MONEY FOR IT?

YES. IT'S A PLEDGE DRIVE. WE'RE TRYING TO RAISE ENOUGH CASH TO PRESERVE IT FOREVERMORE.

GOSH, I WISH I HAD EXTRA CASH TO GIVE YOU, BUT THE ONLY THING I HAVE IS THIS RARE SPECIES OF LEECH.

GIVE IT TO THEM. MAYBE THEY CAN SELL IT.

7/1

OH, DEAR NEPHEW, WOULD YOU BE SO KIND AS TO MAKE THAT CONTRIBUTION?

SURE.

I PLEDGE A LEECH, AUNTS, TO THE FLAKE OF THE UNITED STATES OF AMERICA.

AND HERE'S THE LEECH WHO SUCKS THE FUN OUT OF THE COMICS PAGE.

First off, I am not a leech. Secondly, I put the fun *into* the comics page. So take that, *Blondie* and *Hagar the Horrible*.

216

 Dear everyone who said I wouldn't amount to much in life,

 Please know this.

 Every single day for the last thirty years, I've eaten at least a pound of cheese.

 IT'S NICE TO PROVE THE HATERS WRONG.

I once spoke in Columbus, Ohio, with a number of other cartoonists. After my turn was done, I sat down in the back of the room with a huge block of cheese a fan had given me. I didn't have a knife or a plate, so I just held it with both hands and took bites out of it. I looked pretty classy.

 HEY, RAT... COME OVER HERE... I'D LIKE TO INTRODUCE YOU TO MY CO-WORKER.

 WHAT ARE YOU DOING? / IT'S MY COCKTAIL PARTY PERISCOPE. IT ALLOWS ME TO LOOK STRAIGHT AT SOMEONE'S NAMETAG TO SEE IF THE PERSON'S IMPORTANT OR JUST SOME LOSER WASTING MY TIME.

 I'M SO SORRY. / WHOA. ME TOO. THIS GUY'S A NOBODY.

 WHERE'S GOAT TODAY? / HIS NEIGHBORS' KID IS HAVING A SLUMBER PARTY, SO THEY ASKED GOAT IF HE'D TELL THE KIDS SOME SCARY STORIES.

 OOOOH... WHAT KIND OF SCARY STORIES?

 AND WHEN I WAS A KID, WE ONLY HAD EIGHT CHANNELS.

The best part about having just eight channels (if there was a best part) was that if a show was popular, it was *really* popular. Like with *Happy Days*, you could safely assume the day after it aired that every other kid in your class had seen the same thing you did.

217

I believe Emilio is the only friend I've ever made. And he's not even that smart or interesting. I wish I had chosen better.

Not quite sure why the doctor has his back turned to Rat. You should never turn your back on Rat.

Note from Stephan: This is my sister, Parisa. She lives far from me.

(Caricatures not my strength.)

She has a certain set of opinions on government, taxes, immigration, and the environment.

YAP YAP YAP YAP.

I do not share any of those opinions.

That becomes apparent the one or two times a year we see each other.

YOU LOON

ARGUE ARGUE ARGUE ARGUE

But then—and here's the weird part—after about an hour of disagreeing, something happens.

We realize we agree on a few things.

I think that makes sense.

You do?

Which makes us realize one more thing.

That each of the outlets we normally rely upon for news makes MONEY by creating CONFLICT.

So sometimes turn them off.

And talk to your sister.

Okay, irrespective of politics, I think you're a loon.

That's fair.

7/8

All true. Though her arms and legs aren't sticks.

Well, I guess the thumbs-up could be acceptable. Depending on the mother.

That woman has stick legs. Maybe she's related to my sister Parisa.

I now get up at least once a night to relieve myself. And anecdotes like that are what makes your purchase of this book worthwhile.

An actual law of physics. I saw it on that whiteboard at MIT before I erased everything and drew Rat.

HEY, THOMAS—IF YOU'RE READING THIS, ANSWER MY TEXTS OR I WILL TELL MOM TO TAKE AWAY ALL THOSE CHEETOS YOU EAT.

Not all comedy needs to be sophisticated. Sometimes you can just sit on a baby.

[Note from Stephan's editor, Lucas Wetzel, in regard to the last comment: Do not actually sit on a baby.]

WHAT ARE YOU DOING, GOAT?

THIS FASCINATING THOUGHT EXERCISE WHERE YOU WRITE DOWN THE THREE PEOPLE FROM HISTORY THAT YOU'D MOST LIKE TO GO TO DINNER WITH.

CAN I TRY?

SURE.

1) Someone who pays.
2) Someone who pays.
3) Someone who pays.

WHY IS THAT FASCINATING?

Dear Pigita, I'm sorry that sometimes I'm too naive.

DUDE, YOU NEED TO PUT AN UMLAUT OVER THE 'I' IN 'NAÏVE.'

naïve.

UMLAUT, NOT OMELETTE.

NOW I'M HUNGRY.

I was afraid people wouldn't know that was an omelette, so I had Rat say it in the last panel. That was smart, because now I think it's a burrito.

CHOMP CHOMP CHOMP

RRRING RRRING

HELLO?

HI. THIS IS ACME TIME-SHARES WITH A GREAT OFFER ONLY FOR YOU!

BUT I'M EATING DINNER.

THIS WILL ONLY TAKE A MINUTE OF YOUR—

☆CLICK☆

KABOOM

'EXPLODE A TELEMARKETER' IS A VERY USEFUL APP.

I'm not sure *what* food that is. Let's call it fettuccine.

BOOKSHELF ASSEMBLY INSTRUCTIONS

**(1) Identify the parts:
3 shelves
2 side panels**

(2) Attach right side panel with four screws provided.

(3) Realize one screw doesn't fit. Force it. Split wood.

7/22

(4) Swear. Kick things. Blame spouse for everything.

MAYBE WE SHOULD DO SOMETHING ELSE THIS SUNDAY.

GO AHEAD. BLAME ME.

I cannot build one thing. I am not exaggerating. If one thing has to be assembled, I throw it across the room and hope for the best.

I wear headphones when I go to cafés to protect me from this harrowing menace.

I forget names like crazy. I know mine and usually my wife's.

We have an HOA where my studio is, and they made us put in a whole new driveway. And thus, the HOA character was born.

These strips are the price I exact for making me put in a new driveway.

227

It's funny how sometimes these scribbly little drawings (like the monster in this case) can be more effective than my regular drawings. They seem to just have more life.

Dear Pigita,
You are the light of my life. The wind beneath my wings. The reason for my existence.

YOU DUMB PIG. GIRL-FRIENDS DON'T WANT TRITE PHRASES. THEY WANT YOU TO TALK FROM THE HEART. USE YOUR OWN WORDS.

You are better than tacos.

GO WITH TRITE PHRASES.

ACTUALLY, TACOS MIGHT WIN.

AND THIS ROOM HERE IS THE LIVING ROOM.

LIVING ROOM? WHAT'S A LIVING ROOM?

FOR SALE

IT'S MORE OF A FANCY ROOM FOR WHEN YOU WANT TO FORMALLY ENTERTAIN GUESTS.

AH. HOW USEFUL.

IF IT WAS 1890!

MAYBE THIS HOUSE ISN'T FOR YOU.

SERIOUSLY, COULD IT BE MADE INTO A SPORTS BAR?

The living room of my studio has a pool table, pinball machine, and dartboard. It's the best living room ever.

HEY, GOAT, RAT AND I WERE WONDERING... WHAT'S THE BEST WAY TO SUCCEED IN LIFE? IS IT LUCK? TIMING?

YOU KNOW, PIG, IT REALLY JUST COMES DOWN TO A WILLINGNESS TO WORK HARDER THAN OTHERS.

WE'RE SCREWED.

That's supposed to be an ocean on the other side of the wall. But you'd never know it. So I'm telling you now.

We have this rock in our backyard that's half-embedded in the ground. Lately, I've been sledgehammering it. It feels really good.

Stupid HOA. Never should have made me fix that stupid driveway.

Those graduation caps really are perfect for collecting money. Maybe that's why they're made that way.

An employee of Nike who is also a fan of the strip once gave me a really cool tour of the Nike campus in Beaverton, Oregon. I got to see the beat-up old waffle iron that was the inspiration for the sole of the first Nike shoe.

Restaurants that bill themselves as "legendary" rarely are. How do I know that? Because I am the legendary Stephan Pastis.

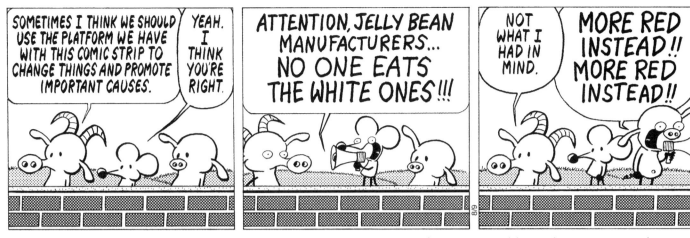

Seriously, who eats the white ones? They are always the last ones left. I'm gonna blame the same guy who puts coconut filling in chocolate candy.

I spent a good part of 2018 filming the *Timmy Failure* movie in Canada. Their spelling thus made its way into the strip.

For some reason, I gave every person in this strip a nose, except Jojo. So I guess he couldn't smell the dragon coming. Oh well. He's dead now.

Here, Goat says he had only seven channels when he was young. But in the earlier July 4 strip, he said he had eight channels. So Goat is a big, fat liar.

For my kids' birthdays, I make them birthday cards like this. Some have dead clowns. Some have alcoholics. I'm a pretty good dad.

HEY, RAT, MY FRIEND THE TURKEY IS ON THE PHONE.

THE ONE WHO MOVED TO THE ARCTIC?

YEAH, HIS FEATHERS DON'T KEEP HIM WARM AT ALL. ANYWAYS, HE HEARD YOU GAVE UP BEER AND WANTED TO KNOW IF IT WAS GRADUAL OR ALL OF A SUDDEN.

SUDDEN.

COLD TURKEY, COLD TURKEY.

YOU MAKE ME WANT TO DRINK AGAIN.

WHAT ARE YOU DOING, PIG?

RAT SAYS MY PRONUNCIATION OF WORDS IS OFF. SO HE GAVE ME SOME WORDS TO PRACTICE.

WELL, THAT WAS NICE OF HIM. WHAT WORDS DID HE GIVE YOU TO PRACTICE?

— EYE
— YAM
— FLAT
— CHEW
— LEANT

SO MATURE.

HEY, WHERE IS EVERYONE GOING?

For those who are too mature to get this, those words form the sentence, "I am flatulent."

HEY, RAT, THIS IS MY PAL, PETEY THE PERMANENTLY OFFENDED GUY.

WHAT'S HE YELLING ABOUT?

OH, I'M NOT YELLING. IT'S JUST THAT IF YOU SPEND YOUR WHOLE LIFE GETTING OFFENDED, YOUR FACE AND ARM EVENTUALLY FREEZE LIKE THIS.

WHAT A JOY YOU MUST BE AT PARTIES.

OKAY, **NOW** I'M OFFENDED!

I never know what to say to someone who writes me to say how offended they were by a strip. Maybe, "How interesting!" Or, "Way to go!"

ELLY ELEPHANT WROTE IN HER DIARY. 	*Dear diary, I want a boyfriend.* 	*One I can go out with once a week.* 
Who is quiet but impactful. 	*Solid but fun.* 	*Who expects nothing but never cheats.*  

And above all, gives me space.

8/19

Almost like I can just take him when I want him and put him away when I don't. 	**ELLY ELEPHANT REALIZED SHE HAD JUST DESCRIBED A BOWLING BALL.** 	**ELLY LIVED HAPPILY EVER AFTER.** 

I have sat here staring at this strip for a good 15 minutes and I cannot think of a single thing to say about it. So I'm gonna leave a big blank space and ask you to fill in something yourself:

_____

_____

_____

_____

Have you ever once in your life clicked on the "review details" button? I certainly haven't. Who knows what's in there?

The newspaper comics page is filled with a lot of sappy family strips. *Pearls* provides an alternative perspective.

I really like this strip because it pretty accurately sums up what I think about complainers.

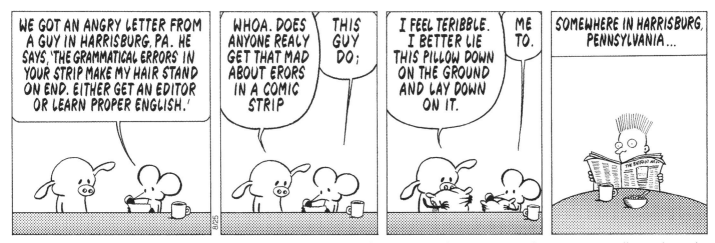

In 2016, a reader of the *Patriot-News* newspaper in Harrisburg, Pennsylvania, wrote the paper to call *Pearls* "sick" and "disgusting." So I thought I'd give a shout-out to Harrisburg here.

It seems like we are a bit divided.

You @#@#*@ Weasel.

@*@#*# YOU!

So here's some advice from everyone's favorite Rat...

Yell louder, because volume convinces.

@#*!

@*@#*

@#*!!

@#*!

OHH.... I SEE YOUR POINT.

Insult more, because disrespect opens hearts.

Scum!

Jerk!

Loser.

Awwww

And listen to more of the shows that made you hate everyone. Because that helps.

THEY'RE MORONS!

ARRGH YES! YES! YES!

8/26

For as they say, 'DIVIDED, WE THRIVE.'

IT'S 'DIVIDED, WE FALL.'

OH... WELL, I WAS CLOSE.

I WILL INSULT YOU 'TIL I CONVINCE YOU!!

In the old days when I did these Rat-drawn strips, the panel boxes were as neat and straight as my own. But then I realized that was a mistake. If Rat were drawing the strip, he would also be drawing the panel boxes. So now I make them messy.

Story of my life. I say just that one remark too many. No wonder I spend so much time alone.

Half of the *Timmy Failure* movie was filmed in Portland, Oregon, a town replete with hipsters. So I just looked out the window and drew what I saw.

I remember back in grade school we had one day a year where a doctor would look at us and check our heads for lice. I'm proud to say I was lice-free.

Ah, Portland. I miss you.

242

The way you know that's Mark Zuckerberg in the second to last panel is that he says he is Mark Zuckerberg. Maybe I should do caricatures for a living. I could just draw a stick figure with a speech balloon saying, "I am _____" and fill in their name.

Thought I Had as an Adult but Never Once Had as a Kid: How dumb is it that at children's birthday parties, we put one kid at the center of a circle of other kids, spin him around, blindfold him, and let him loose with a baseball bat?

Do any gyms actually do this? It seems like it really could generate a lot of power over the course of a day.

244

My Aunt Leah had a couch like this. On summer days, it really hurt if you stood up quickly.

Instead of that dumb "555" number, I should have put in my best friend Emilio's cell number. Then you could all call him day and night.

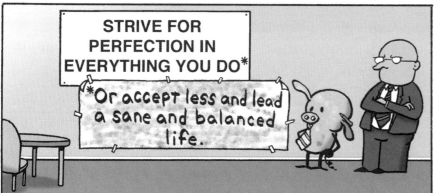

I was in Spain a month ago and they really seemed to have mastered the relaxed, balanced life. Stores close from 2 p.m. to 5 p.m. so people can nap. Which is great, unless you need something from a store at 3:30 p.m. Then you want to yell and punch someone in the face.

HEY, PACO PIÑATA, HOW GOES IT?

TERRIFIC. I FINALLY REALIZED I'VE LET MYSELF GET TOO PESSIMISTIC. BUT NO MORE. THIS IS GONNA BE A GREAT WEEK!

WHAM WHAM WHAM

AND I THOUGHT I HAD BAD MONDAYS.

When we were kids, my best friend Emilio was much stronger than the rest of us. So at his birthday parties, he'd always be the one to actually break apart the piñata. But by the time he got the blindfold off, all the rest of us had made off with the candy. I'm a pretty good best friend.

I JUST HAD A THOUGHT.

WHAT'S THAT?

MAYBE WHEN WE JUDGE PEOPLE ON THE INTERNET, WE DON'T KNOW EVERYTHING.

WHOA. THAT MAKES ME STOP AND WONDER.

WONDER WHAT?

WHY THAT WOULD POSSIBLY MATTER.

GOOD POINT. HANG 'EM HIGH!

I can't believe the number of stories on social media lately where everyone gets very outraged about something only to learn 24 hours later that the story was not accurate. Newspapers might not get everything right, but at least they have standards for what stories they print.

HI. I THINK THE STOCK MARKET IS DOING VERY WELL AND I'D LIKE TO INVEST EVERYTHING I HAVE.

TERRIFIC. IT'S GOING GANGBUSTERS AND YOU'D BE A FOOL NOT TO INVEST.

FINANCIAL ADVISORS

BLIP

FINANCIAL ADVISORS

WHAT WAS THAT?

MARKET CORRECTION. YOU LOST EVERYTHING.

FINANCIAL ADVISORS

REMIND ME NEVER TO SAVE MONEY.

SMART PEOPLE SPEND IT ALL ON BEER.

If Pig is walking past a window, it pretty much guarantees it will later be involved in the joke (as in the second panel, where he looks out and sees the fencers). These days, I really try to not add any unnecessary details because 1) simple is better; and 2) I am lazy.

If someone is given a new identity and put in the witness protection program, how do they avoid reflexively turning around when someone calls their original name? Because if someone yelled "Stephan!" I'd turn around and instantly be shot by mobsters.

248

GOVERNMENT 101

WILL THIS BE ON THE FINAL?

Let's call giant campaign contributions what they are.

They are bribes.

Have a bribe. | Campaign Contribution.

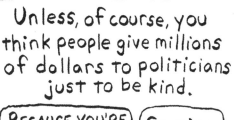

Unless, of course, you think people give millions of dollars to politicians just to be kind.

BECAUSE YOU'RE YOU. | So nice.

So what does that mean for you?

We're screwed? | Good guess.

That means that even if 80% of the American people support a bill, it often can't pass because the money holds your Congressman hostage.

YOU WILL SIT HERE AND DO NOTHING. | CAN I WHISTLE? | YOU CAN WHISTLE.

9/16

But don't despair.

☹

Because there's a way to fix it.

☺

Become a billionaire.

Because you're you. | So nice

I WAS THINK-ING GET THE MONEY OUT OF POLITICS. | BECOMING A BILLIONAIRE IS EASIER. | DANCE, SENATOR, DANCE!

I like this strip, but I just realized I screwed something up. The first eight panels of the strip are supposed to have been drawn by Rat, and yet, the first panel has a drawing of Rat and Pig that has clearly been drawn by me. These things happen.

Fun Fact: I'm 6' 1" tall and weigh 195 pounds. But when I was 16, I was the same height and just 125 pounds. Between my age and the fact that I ran cross-country, I could eat just about anything and not gain weight.

This strip has confused even me. It's probably bad when myself confuses myself.

Insider Knowledge You Didn't Care to Know, but Now Will: Goat is almost always drinking tea. Thus, the string of his tea bag is hanging out of his mug. No other character drinks tea.

Next week I have to buy a new car so I can give my old Honda Accord to my son. SO, THOMAS, START ANSWERING MY TEXTS OR YOU WILL BE DRIVING AROUND IN A LITTLE RED WAGON.

Goat: Tea bag. Pig: No tea bag. You can now draw *Pearls* yourself.

PLAN FOR LIFE

Establish own
business.
Make millions.
Retire happy.

PLAN FOR LIFE

THAT'S A GREAT GOAL. AND IF YOU'RE WILLING TO WORK LONG HOURS AT IT EVERY DAY OF THE WEEK AND GIVE IT EVERYTHING YOU HAVE, YOU CAN MAKE IT HAPPEN.

PLAN FOR LIFE

PLAN FOR LIFE

Eat cheese
and
hope for
the best.

I think my syndicate is going to put the last panel of this strip on a coffee mug.

AND SO, YOU'D CALL FOR ONE, AND SOMETIMES THEY'D SHOW UP, AND SOMETIMES THEY WOULDN'T. YOU COULDN'T TRACK THEM. AND EVEN IF THEY DID SHOW UP THEY OFTEN SMELLED AND THE COST WAS ALWAYS A SURPRISE.

AND WHAT DID YOU CALL THESE THINGS AGAIN?

TAXI CABS.

PARDON ME, SIR, BUT YOU HAD THE MOST HELLISH UPBRINGING EVER.

WE DIDN'T HAVE ☺☆#⑥☆⑥# SMARTPHONES!!

I was recently in Eugene, Oregon, and for some reason they did not allow ridesharing apps in the city. It was weird trying to hail a cab again. Even weirder was my Airbnb, which promised an outdoor hot tub that turned out to be a bathroom tub buried in the dirt.

WHAT ARE YOU DOING, PIG?

I'M TAKING A CONFLICTS COURSE... IT TEACHES YOU HOW TO DEAL WITH OTHER PEOPLE. HERE, TAKE THE QUIZ WITH ME.

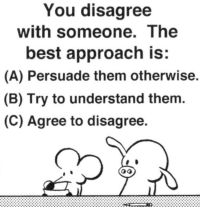

You disagree with someone. The best approach is:

(A) Persuade them otherwise.

(B) Try to understand them.

(C) Agree to disagree.

D) Punch them in the head.

THAT ONE WAS EASY.

I burn a lot of bridges myself. So Flame-O McGibbons is a pretty good friend of mine.

I see Rat as the star of *Pearls*, but Pig is really the heart and soul of it.

9/30

Ooh, great strip to end the book on. Approval by the Word Police.
And with that endorsement, I'll see you in the next treasury.

CinemaScope in Eastman COLOR

El Desperado de Santa Rosa

Starring *Stephan Pastis*

© 2020 Stephan Pastis

Andrews McMeel
PUBLISHING®
www.andrewsmcmeel.com

A *Pearls Before Swine* Production

"An embarrassment to cinema." —Film Critic Tim Lynch

"I found myself rooting for the theater to burn down." —Film Historian Lucas Wetzel